closed wounds open hands

Rediscovering a Saviour with Scars

Eleasha,
You are a beautiful
woman after God's own
heart. Never stop.
Kerri

Kerri Lynn Jerema

CLOSED WOUNDS, OPEN HANDS

Printed in Canada

Print ISBN: 978-1-4866-1960-3
eBook ISBN: 978-1-4866-1961-0

Word Alive Press
119 De Baets Street, Winnipeg, MB R2J 3R9
www.wordalivepress.ca

WORD ALIVE PRESS

FSC www.fsc.org MIX Paper from responsible sources FSC® C016245

Cataloguing in Publication may be obtained through Library and Archives Canada

To Samuel.

Your constant love has confirmed my emerging suspicion that God's love is forever beyond my mind's ability to grasp it.

Contents

Chapter One

it all starts with the fall

A slight wobble left,
I overcompensate right.
Flesh colliding with concrete
tears His face from my sight.

I'm left surveying the fallout,
body split open, blood spilled.
In my mess a mirrored reflection
of His promise wholly fulfilled.

Each movement is painful.
I am frozen with fear.
My sense of direction—now altered.
What once was sure—unclear.

I'm reaching down to get up
and up to get down,
held within His backwards paradigm,
where the lost are sought and found.

The warm June evening hangs in the house long after everyone is asleep. I am readying our son for bed as I do every night; he is almost four, but all kinds of old already. The two of us take comfort in the routine we go through faithfully and meticulously each night, right down to the five-step process involved in teeth brushing: bottom first, spit, top next, spit, then a swipe of his lips with the hand towel. After a quick kiss to the crown of his head, it takes little effort to convince my young worker man to find his bed because every night, like clockwork, we save the best for last: story time.

As I lower myself onto his loudly decorated bed sheets, I smile at the patterns boasting hammers, drills, and all the earthly pleasures he already craves. My worker man is absolutely convinced that he holds a full-time job. Each day, he jumps out of bed to dress his mere three-foot frame from head to toe in highly visible construction gear. From the tip of his yellow hard hat to the soles of his steal toe waterproof work boots, my worker man is set to begin his day, which often includes tightening kitchen cabinet screws, hauling wood across the back lawn, and hammering loose playhouse nails.

Although children are born without instruction manuals and numbered parts, from my experience, every part and parcel of their being is present from that first hallowed cry. Rather than learning to read a manual, we learn to read our children—the expressions that alert us to their oncoming emotions, the idiosyncrasies that reveal when their needs are not being met, the way they absorb the world with zero ability to filter out stimuli—it's no wonder the first few years of life are filled with many tears. Miraculously, with adequate love and prayerful guidance, the assembly of a child takes place in the mere blink of a mother's eye. Too often, we realize that our parental tweaking has either helped or hindered our child's ability to function in the world only after their assembly is complete.

I ponder this thought: that God has willingly bestowed on me the privilege of overseeing the manufacturing of His intricate design. It's a serious job title, one that requires holy endurance to make it to the last page of the manual.

My son's head finds its way into the warm crook of my neck. During his decent, our cheeks brush, and I notice that his are still dewy from the bath. I drink in the sacredness of this moment slowly, intentionally. The busyness of the day is quietly swallowed up in the tight space between us. I feel my edges, sharpened by the day's demands, begin to round. My nostrils brim with the sweet scent of innocence.

My young worker man breaks the silence a little too quickly for my liking, "Just *onnnnne* more story from your head, Mom?"

Although I can't see his eyes, I know they have commenced their dance, big and wide, just like his daddy's. I've never seen eyes change their demeanour the way they do in my boy's. One minute they're dark and deep, full of anger or sorrow, and then, in the same way a sky clears after a storm, they lighten to a completely new shade of delicate brown.

I melt.

"Okay, one more story." I reply. "Do you want it to be about you as a little boy or me as a little girl?"

"You, Mom," he grins. "And make it good."

He adjusts his position, and, all at once, my attention becomes hyper focused on the physicality of the body resting its weight on me. This is the body for which I pleaded with God and, in His divine mercy, the one I birthed. From the very moment of his grand entrance, my son's body required me to meet a host of physical needs, from nursing and burping, to rocking to sleep. And just as my flesh opened wide to accommodate his life, his existence had opened our hearts to joy and pain. Holding his body in my hands connects me to every experience we've shared. I've locked them away in my heart like Mary did with her small babe (Luke 2:19).

My worker man tugs on my arm, begging me to return to my storytelling duties. In my mind, I flip through the stories of my youth like files, intentionally tucked away yet easily accessible—the ones I've already told, the ones I'm saving, and the ones that are only for him. I pause when my fingers finally pull up the file I've been searching for. I begin.

"Mommy was about six years old, and I was biking to school with my brother, Uncle Brian."

I've barely started speaking and he interjects, "What kind of bike?"

I smile at his eagerness and reply, "It was red and small, with a white basket out front and delicate flowers printed along the sides. I had only just learned and so I was still a bit... wobbly."

"Wobbly?" His chest rises and falls, and I can almost feel waves of enjoyment radiating out of his skin.

"You know, not very solid on my wheels just yet, still learning," I answer.

He nods, but the understanding has not yet sunk in. "Okay, keep going."

Now I am the one to adjust, my eyes closing. Although I am thirty-two, the memory feels vivid and fresh, still tender.

"I was riding behind my brother, and he was going faster than me, just barely. I could feel the gap between us widening, and I didn't like that."

I've always been competitive, fiercely so, and I know my marrow runs thick inside my worker man's bones. He barrels down slides and darts to swings, always racing, always attempting to find his place on the podium. It is a blessing and a curse—I am too painfully aware.

"Slowly, but surely, I am falling behind Uncle Brian. I'm racing to catch him and all of a sudden my wheel strikes a stone."

"Do you jolt? Like Jim?" he asks. He's remembering a story we read about Jim who jolts off his bike. His body, tense with excitement, can't help but anticipate what's coming next.

"Yes, the bike jolts and then throws me off, and I crash hard into the pavement. My knee hits first and it hits hard," I say. I remember the blood that flowed out of my knee onto the ground, as alarming as it was fascinating.

I continue, "Uncle Brian must have heard my scream and hammered on his brakes because, when I look up, he's right beside me."

"Did it hurt?" he asks while squirming in my embrace. This worker man knows falling.

"Oh yes, I couldn't walk on it at first. It was bleeding so bad that Uncle Brian scooped me up in his arms and carried me all the way back to our house."

I wait for his string of questions to break the silence. Instead, the room remains quiet and his body still. I look down to see his eyes gazing up at his ceiling. It is clear my worker man is digesting the feast he has just been fed. First, he moves around the different textures, sorting out what he likes and what he does not. Next, he absorbs the nutrients, passing on what he considers waste. Finally, he savours the taste this story has left in his mouth.

Does anything beat a good story? It is an avenue our brains can both participate in and observe. We dive into the story when it suits and exemplifies us, yet we are allowed to exit anytime we'd rather quietly contemplate the characters' actions or fate. I am so thankful the Bible is truth told through story and that Jesus knew the captivating power behind deliberately crafted tales.

We both lie still in the moment a little while longer, our bodies close and our hearts closer. I turn to kiss both of his rosy checks, flush with fatigue.

He exhales before his husky voice says, "I love you, Mom. All the way to the moon and all the way back."

These words stand tall, towering over the stresses of my day. If I could somehow find my way back to this moment during times of monumental frustration, I'd be different—I'd be better.

"I know, Son. I love you that way too," I whisper while cradling his body in mine. We end the night by saying simple, heartfelt prayers before he drifts to sleep.

Long after I have left his bed, the story I've told lingers in my mind, jostling it's way through my conscious thoughts. The girl on the bike, pedalling ferociously, chasing after something she couldn't quite attain. And the fall. Skin hitting pavement, flesh tearing as it grinds against the grainy surface of the road. Wasn't this the perfect metaphor for my life? All thirty-two years of it? Every full-fledged pursuit of reckless abandon disguised under the false belief that, once the gap between reality and desire closed, I'd be fulfilled. First the chase, followed by the fall, and then the wound.

The part of the story I left out for fear that I'd stir the anxious seed nestled inside my young son's heart was that I had missed the class field trip the day after my accident. I was stuck at school under the care of my brother and his teacher while my classmates frolicked at the park, oblivious to the pain my misfortune had cost me. A fall at high speeds rarely occurs without consequence. I stare down at my bare knees that have been browned by the blazing summer sun. It's still there all these years later—a scar. I circle my finger around the faint outline of the wound from years past, blemished skin that has grown and stretched through years of toil and child-rearing.

A haphazard Wikipedia search pulls up a description of a scar as an "area of fibrous connective tissue that replaces normal skin after injury."[1] Quite simply, the skin you once had is gone forever. In its place is a new kind of flesh covering, one that is thick and smooth to the touch with a shimmering pink coating that alerts the eye and stirs the mind. Even though scarring is a natural part of our body's healing process, there is something inherently unfamiliar and mildly unnerving about it.

When our daughter was eight months old, she lost her balance while supporting herself on one of our blunt-ended IKEA coffee tables in the living room. The weight of her sixteen-pound body collapsing all at once on her chin forced a tiny tooth to tear straight through her tender pink lip. While we were waiting in the emergency room for the doctor to stitch her up, the question I kept asking the nurses, the doctors, and my husband was, "Will she be okay?" But that's not what I meant. The fear echoing off the walls of my heart was, "Will it scar?"

Why do I cringe at the very thought of my daughter's permanently altered lip? Perhaps it is because I was conceived remembering a life void of change and consequence. When God knit me together in utter seclusion, He did it with hands that only knew divine perfection. Therefore, given such flawless entry into human existence, every wounding becomes a painful reminder that, due to sin, our bodies are being held against their will in bondage to decay (Romans 8:21). It's in the creaking of stiff joints and the shuffling of faltering feet that we audibly hear our bodies groan to be returned to their intended form. The deterioration of my body, or any unwelcomed change to it, although commonplace in our world, will always feel unnatural and solicit within me a visceral response.

But is it merely my flesh that cries out in anguish against these unpleasantries? Or is there something inherently intertwined, yet altogether different at work within me?

Genesis records God's creation of humanity as follows: "*Then the Lord God formed the man of dust from the ground and breathed into his nostrils the breath of life and the man became a living creature*" (Genesis 2:7).

God first moulded our physical bodies from the dust, enabling us to see, and hear, and touch, and smell, and taste, all of which are necessary for us to interact with and fully appreciate His created world. However, that was not all our triune God had in mind for us. In order for us to engage in a dynamic, living relationship with Him, we needed to be made in His glorious image (Genesis 1:27). What comes next in the creation narrative is proof of a multidimensional human existence. God breathed His Spirit into humanity, igniting another entity within us—a soul! It is the equation of a body plus a soul that makes us a complete creation.

Just as God's three separate entities, Father, Son, and Holy Spirit, work in harmony to commune with us, our bodies and souls work together to enable us to carry out a relationship with His divine being. And in much the same way that Father, Son, and Holy Spirit consistently carry out the work of the Father, our bodies and souls enable us to fulfill our created purpose—namely, to glorify God. Paul calls attention to this when he says, *"Now may the God of peace himself sanctify you completely, and may your whole spirit and soul and body be kept blameless at the coming of our Lord Jesus Christ"* (1 Thessalonians 5:23).

Even though our physical and spiritual states are separate, they remain inextricably woven together. Our understanding of the soul can greatly inform our understanding of our physical bodies, just as our experiences with our physical bodies can give us greater insight into our souls. And, as we experience God differently through the Father, Son, or Holy Spirit, He is able to communicate distinctly with our physical bodies *and* our souls in order to make Himself known to us.

As I listen from my position on the couch, my worker man's tossing and turning slows into a deep laborious snore. My hands feel blindly around the same IKEA side table that bore the brunt of our daughter's injury until my fingertips brush familiar leather skin. I open the Word to Genesis, where Moses recounts Jacob's experience of falling. His story is also one of a physical struggle that mirrored an internal battle. It involves God reaching out to him by communicating with the entity he can perceive—his body—so that he could become attuned to the dysfunction of the entity that remains unseen—his soul. I turn the story around in my mind, examining it from different angles like a precious gem. It's Jacob's story, but it's also mine.

Jacob's life was rife with physical struggle from the moment of his conception. After wrestling with his twin brother in the womb of his mother, Rachel, Jacob entered the world grasping at his bother's heel (Genesis 25:26). He wanted to be first. Only seconds old and his soul had tasted the bitter cup of failure.

Later in his life, Jacob, whose name means "one who supplants" or "over-thrower," succumbed to deceit in order to win his father's blessing. Jacob so desperately wanted to control his own destiny that he allowed the desires of the flesh to outweigh obedience to the spirit.

I pause my reading and search for the shiny, pink scar on my knee. This brand transports me back to the girl on the bike, the one clamouring for control at the wheel, the one who believed that being first was ultimately best—the girl grasping at the heel. How many times would I fall before I realized I too was focusing on my physical being, glorifying dust over the very breath of God?

Pulling my thoughts back to Moses's words, I smile at the way God does not abandon His rebellious child, Jacob. In fact, God seeks him out.

It is the evening before Jacob is about to encounter his estranged brother, Esau. He has sent his wife and children away from the camp, possibly preparing for the worst possible outcome. In the dead of the night, God sends a celestial being to the camp to engage Jacob in a physical quarrel. Here is a man who has allowed his flesh to guide his decisions for far too long, causing him injury and pain, yet God meets Jacob on a palpable level—the physical. While Jacob rolls around in the dirt, he remains unaware that God wants to extend to him a spiritual blessing that will heal the wounds he's tried to redeem unsuccessfully through the flesh.

God is patient with Jacob, allowing the struggle, perhaps even letting his persistence be exercised. And then the celestial being delivers a life-altering blow to Jacob's hip, knocking it out of its socket. The metaphor God writes into Jacob's narrative cries out for those clinging to the Word to search for the treasure buried in it. The upturning of dirt reveals God's reason for choosing Jacob's hip: the hip joint is the "largest, strongest joint in the human body."[2] Jacob, the one straining to be first, has to be broken down at the strongest part of his physical body so that God may illuminate the wound pride has inflicted on the enduring aspect of his being—his soul.

And it works. Despite the catastrophic physical blow, Jacob clings to the celestial being and cries out, "*I will not let you go unless you bless me*" (Genesis 32:26). The eyes of Jacob's soul have finally been opened through the physical smearing of mud, just like the miracle Jesus once performed (John 9:11). All at once, Jacob can see with eternal perspective that putting his trust in anything besides God will ultimately fail him. What Jacob needs more than physical strength and earthy accomplishments is steadfast faith in a sovereign God.

Jacob's story provides for us a window into the heart of our creator. Our God, who intricately crafted our physical bodies with the ability to re-grow skin after being wounded, also created our souls with a plan for their healing and redemption. But here our bodies do not totally reflect our souls. The Bible tells us our physical bodies have been given an expiration date, but our souls will live forever (1 Corinthians 15:42).

I see evidence of this truth exercised through Jesus' short ministry on earth. Jesus spent a considerable amount of his ministry caring for physical bodies. Matthew records one such event in his account of Jesus' works, saying, *"A vast crowd brought to him people who were lame, blind, crippled, those who couldn't speak, and many others. They laid them before Jesus, and he healed them all"* (Matthew 15:30, NLT). Jesus concerned himself with our bodies, even though He knew they were temporary. Why? Thankfully for us, Jesus answered this question when a group of religious leaders questioned him for healing a paralyzed man on the Sabbath. Jesus said his reason for healing this man was "*...that you may know that the Son of Man has authority on earth to forgive sins...*" (Matthew 9:6). Jesus' self-proclaimed purpose in healing bodies was to prove that He had the authority to accomplish the mission from his Father—to heal souls.

If Jesus' chief mission on earth was to heal physical bodies, it would seem He failed miserably. How many men lurked just beyond the borders of His audiences, cast out by society and unable to reach Him? How many women dreamt of grasping His garment that they might be made well, yet had no way of parting through the crowds? How many children lay motionless in their beds, the sound of their mother's wailing heard deep into the night, while the saviour moved from town to town without a place to rest his head? Does this thought not spew forth emotions today? How could a good God miraculously heal some and not others? This question has caused many who believed to turn away from the truth because the answer does not exempt anyone from physical and spiritual suffering.

Our society seems more fixated on the first type of suffering than the second. We often pray for our kids, our extended family, and our friends to be kept out of harm's way, yet seldom do we pray for sin to be confessed, for secrets to be exposed, or for the Lord's discipline to rain down. Although the scriptures prove that our physical bodies moved Jesus with compassion, it also seems clear that they were not His primary concern. The crucifixion of Jesus' own earthly body points to a further reaching, all-encompassing healing available to anyone who asks—spiritual healing or healing of the soul.

Our house is nearly seventy years old, and I've learned a few things about cracks since we bought it six years ago. At first glance, cracks can seem rather insignificant, barely noticeable to the naked eye. Nonetheless, over time, one crack gives birth to three more cracks, and soon your husband is hammering away at solid concrete to demolish your entire front step because it can no longer hold itself up under the pressure. Cracks are problematic.

The fault lines where my own soul cracked created space and soil for the adversary to plant his deceptive seed. In time, that seed sprouted weed after weed, splitting the earth of my soul with fear, where faith ought to be growing and bearing fruit.

I think back to the girl on the bike and that first fall—the crack of hard pavement against my physical body. Like Jacob, it would take a physical wrestling match with God for me to discover I had been limping through life with an injured soul. Like Jacob, I focused on the physical part of me that cracked before I noticed the fractures in my soul. And, just as my knee lost its functionality after my fall, I needed to face the hard truth that my soul was not operating the way my creator had designed it to.

Jacob is moved by this same revelation, for he does not beg God to heal his hip. Rather, knuckles clenched around the celestial being he's warring with, Jacob calls out for God's blessing and spiritual healing, that the functionality of his soul may be restored. At last, Jacob's sight aligns with God's will, which Paul reiterates in his second letter to the Corinthians:

So we do not lose heart. Though our outer self is wasting away, our inner self is being renewed day by day. For this light momentary affliction is preparing for us an eternal weight of glory beyond all comparison. As we look not to the things that are seen but to the things that are unseen. For the things that are seen are transient, but the things that are unseen are eternal.

—2 Corinthians 4:16–18

Jacob becomes attuned to the part of his being that will forever beat in unison with Christ, the part of him that things of the earth can never extinguish. His eyes are finally, wholly, fixed on things eternal. His physical state is in the periphery of this new unclouded view. And as Jacob reaches for God in a climactic moment of this story, the narrator writes Himself into the solution and graciously reaches back. God gives Jacob the blessing he is after and binds together the wounds that once marred his soul. The symbolic package this gift comes wrapped in is a new name: "*…Your name shall not longer be called Jacob, but Israel, for you have striven with God and with men, and have prevailed*" (Genesis 32:28).

This may seem odd or insignificant. However, if you wade through the entire Bible, you will see that this pattern repeats itself in the scriptures time and time again. Abraham, Sarah, (Jacob) Israel, Peter, and Paul all receive new names after a holy encounter that changes the trajectory of their life. In every one of these experiences, God uses physical circumstances to refocus their sight on the eternal, thus breathing healing into their souls.

The prophet Isaiah foretold of a saviour who would come to earth to craft, from the mire, new things (Isaiah 43:19). He prophesied that God's holy city "*…shall be called by a new name…*" (Isaiah 62:2). This is a God who is confident in His workmanship and is inviting us to share in the hope that, when our souls hit hard pavement and life seems to come to a screeching halt, His work is just getting started. And we can be sure that He will finish the good work He starts (Philippians 1:6), even if it means we must crack. Because, just maybe, we are one hard fall and a celestial wrestling match away from our greatest blessing—and a new name.

After an evening riddled with doubt and writer's block, I find a place on the couch beside my husband, who is sipping hot tea. I'm wrestling with the reality that I am no theologian and that the truths made known to me through scripture might not be as accurate and fleshed out as well-versed readers may expect. But still—He is calling me to obey, to quiet myself, and to write.

I snuggle close to my husband's familiar warmth and rest my hand upon his strong, broad shoulders. We both crane our necks as we watch our two children frolic in the basement, flitting from one game to the next, content with the very moment they are in and nothing more.

I open my mouth wide and give myself permission to let the fear escape. "What if in my reading and writing I discover someone has already written this book, and done it much better?" I harbour the next thought to myself, afraid of its gripping truth: *Will the exposure, the hurt of beholding my wounds, the humbling of my pride, all be for nothing then*?

My husband turns his head and his eyes carefully search mine, the ones that first held mine ten years ago when we said "I do." His eyes have cast their light on each corner and crevice of my heart, where I once hid my most bitter failures. They have cried with me and for me. I have learned, over time, that I can trust those eyes and the words that are filtered through them.

"Maybe someone has," he says after a thoughtful pause. "But no one will write it like you."

I sure hope he's right.

Chapter Two

the knee-jerk response

Why, when we crack,
do we run for cover?
Our souls shatter.
We slide the veil over.

You call us out;
still we sink down.
You raise us up,
and we covet your crown.

Your truth like a scalpel:
we flee at the thought!
You wound us to heal us;
we're fixed on the cut.

THERE IS A SAYING AS OLD AS THE GRANDFATHER CLOCK THAT USED TO SIT IN my grandmother's living room, which had been passed down through the generations. The saying goes like this: "When bones break, they grow back stronger than before." I'm quite sure I was first told this as a young child, and it became one of those thoughts that stuck like glue. Now, decades after shedding my protective childhood skin, I want to know if this idea is merely used to procure hope in frustrating times or if there is a truth as obvious as the swinging pendulum inside this respective phrase.

I take to the internet to launch my investigation, and my search turns up an article by *The New York Times*: "The Claim: After Being Broken, Bones Can Become Stronger." To my curiosity's delight, it examines the precise phrase I have been deconstructing in my mind.

The article begins by restating popular research known as Wolff's Law, which claims that "bones adapt to pressure or lack of it."[3] In other words, bones have to be used in order to gain strength. I can't help but smile at how this information complements the original hypothesis I keep trying on—that our physical bodies mirror our souls.

James, Christ's own brother, once said it is the "testing of our faith," or the use of our faith, that produces more faith (James 1:3). Paul echos this sentiment in his letter to the Roman church, reminding them that problems or trials give them the blessed opportunity to exercise their faith and trust in God (Romans 5:3).

I continue on in the article and find that it meets, head on, my original question—do bones that break heal stronger than before? My eyes hover over the article's answer in an effort to absorb the words slowly and with certainty. After reading and re-reading the paragraph for what feels like the hundredth time, the air I've been unknowingly holding in slowly escapes through pursed lips. No.

I'm almost angry at this discovery, as if the world has been deceiving everyone with false hope. I read on with dying desire to grasp some kind of visceral truth that will steady my shaky legs. The article quotes Dr. Terry Amaral, who says that "the area that's healing is undergoing rapid mineralization, but because you can't use it, the rest of the bone is demineralized." The article then continues: "As a result, there may be a brief period in the healing process when the fracture site is stronger than the surrounding bone."

Jesus' own words to Paul hit me like the resounding vibrations of a gong: "*...My grace is sufficient for you, for my power is made perfect in weakness...*" (2 Corinthians 12:9).

The very place where our bones crack is stronger only when the rest of the bone is weak. This medical (and physical) truth drips with the authenticity of our soul's breath-giver. God does His best redemptive work in our brokenness when our autonomy, our strength, has been stripped away. This truth is uncomfortable. When juxtaposed with how the world seems to function, weakness equating strength seems counterintuitive. We live in a society that rewards independence and praises self-sufficiency. We condition one another, through the rising emphasis of social media images over face-to-face relationships, to recoil at the sight of injury. Accustomed as we are to scrolling through highlight reels, when we fall we do so forgetting our susceptibility to brokenness. Instead, with hurried hands, we cover up our wounds—God-ordained opportunities to experience His strength—believing they accomplish no good.

I race to finish the article squeezing the remnants of truth onto my parched tongue. The words are plain, and the meaning cannot be construed. Our bones eventually reach "...equal strength, and the fracture site is no more or less likely to break again." There it is. Breaking does not make us stronger in the long run, it simply means at one time we were broken.

I can feel the disappointment tightening every muscle in my body as my heart hammers inside my chest. What hope then can we curate from the inevitability of the fall—our fall? What is the point of suffering through brokenness if it does not, in fact, make us stronger in the long run?

I once again find the physical part of me that was once broken and then healed, no more or less strong, merely altered—the scar on my knee. The creator of the universe who intricately designed starfish with the ability to regrow their own limbs intentionally chose not to give our bodies the capacity to heal without a trace of our own fracture. He could have, but yet, He did not.

I run through the sequence of events that is recalibrating my mind: Falling leads to fracture, and the fracture ushers the surrounding bone into a state of weakness, and only in this moment of weakness can our fracture sites be healed.

This information about our body's healing process flits about in my mind, and I try to catch it and tame its inherent wildness so that I can gaze upon my soul's reflection in it. My first glance looks like this: Breaking removes the stumbling block of our own strength, granting us access to holy strength and focusing our sights on things eternal, which inevitably leads to change. Breaking isn't about building more strength, it's about transformation that can only be ushered in through weakness. Breaking enables us to access the promise of God's healing (Psalm 147:3).

This truth is smeared like lamb's blood all over the door frames of Jesus' short time on earth. Did Jesus not come in physical form to renew our spirits? Was He not adept at intersecting physical circumstance with spiritual change? And what testifies to transformation more powerfully than a scar reminding us of where we were once fractured?

I am reminded of Jesus' words to Thomas: "*...Put your finger here, and see my hands; and put out your hand and place it in my side. Do not disbelieve but believe...*" (John 20:26–27).

Jesus came in the name of holy transformation, knowing the sickness of our human condition that bends us towards doubt. Rather than forsake us when we fell, He came to illustrate for us, physically, what our souls were longing for, spiritually. He harnessed the power of permanently-altered flesh to make the unbelieving, believe. His scars put forth indisputable evidence of the intersection between brokenness and grace, unveiling to us the greatest hope we could possibly imagine—life beyond death—joy despite indescribable pain. Jesus' words to Thomas were penned not just for him, but for nations rife with doubters. Through these words, He shows us that there can be, and often is, a divine purpose for our wounds and our scars. Healing is really about being transformed.

My heart sinks deep into my belly as I am transported, one last time, to the girl on the bike. This was a girl who knew little about these higher thoughts, a girl who did not have her sight fixated on eternal things. I remember, with the vividness of a terrible dream, the fall. When my skin failed to hold up to the force applied against it and it split wide open. I can still feel the stabbing pain and the knee-jerk response that followed less than a second afterwards. Come to think of it—this very response seems second nature each and every time I am injured. My arm sprang forth in record-breaking time to clutch my wound tight and conceal it from my own view and others. I held my hand there a long time, willing my eyes to assess the damage, yet frozen with fear at what I would find.

This may have been my instinctive reaction to a physical wound. However, I am suddenly attuned to the way it mirrors the very first fall of humankind. This fall was not off of a red basket-laden bike, but rather the fall of two unblemished souls.

We are told that Adam and Eve were God's finest creations, made to live and thrive in perfect relationship with Him. They were given one simple mandate to adhere to: "*...You may surely eat of every tree of the garden,* *but of the tree of the knowledge of good and evil you shall not eat, for in the day you eat of it you shall surely die*" (Genesis 2:16–17).

A mere two chapters into the story of creation and any astute reader is bracing herself for impact because God is foreshadowing, like the gifted writer He is, their impending doom. It was not a surprise to Him, yet the fall always seems to catch us off guard. The dormant rebellion lurking inside Adam and Eve is the natural by-product of free will, overpowered by trust in a good Father, that is, until a slithering snake tested Eve's trust and crawled close, belly dragging through dirt, to whisper a vengeful lie, "*...you will not surely die*" (Genesis 3:4).

Reading through this story, we can almost feel the first few wobbles of Adam and Eve's front wheel. It doesn't take much, sudden doubt in the ability of the handlebars to steer them, to cause these two souls to collide with hard, unforgiving concrete. Genesis records the fall as follows:

> *So when the woman saw that the tree was good for food, and that it was a delight to the eyes, and that the tree was to be desired to make one wise, she took of its fruit and ate, and she also gave some to her husband who was with her and he ate. Then the eyes of both were opened, and they knew that they were naked. And they sewed fig leaves together and made themselves loincloths.*
>
> —Genesis 3:6–7

My knee-jerk reaction to cover my injured knee is the same as Adam and Eve's reaction when they look down at the newly-inflicted injury on their souls. Rather than run to their Father and confess what they have done, they hide (Genesis 3:10).

My mind races to connect the dots that seem to be emerging in divine sequence before me. First Jacob, and now Adam and Eve. These are more than stories about people who fall; these stories cut through the very bone and marrow of the human condition. Due to sin, it's only a matter of time before we find ourselves face down with wounded souls. When that happens, we face a crossroads; will we hide or allow ourselves to be transformed?

I didn't know then what I'm just starting to piece together now. Instead of reaching my weary hands up and calling out to the Father who fashioned me for His purposes, knowing my every flaw, I fumbled like a frightened orphan for a place to hide. I ran when God was calling me to stay. I hid when God was bending down low to lift me back up.

Hiding one's injury to the soul has become such an ingrained human condition that it can be a difficult process to articulate. Thankfully, Jesus himself modelled a tried-and-true approach for deconstructing complex topics—storytelling. When explanations seemed insufficient, He turned to truth portrayed through characters, settings, and plot. Although I am not worthy to clasp together one buckle on Jesus' storytelling feet, I have obeyed the call of the Holy Spirit to follow Jesus' example of making truth accessible to people through story. Unlike Jesus' parables, this story I've written is one I survived and now proclaim, like the psalmist: "*Come and hear, all you who fear God, and I will tell you what he has done for my soul*" (Psalm 66:16).

My story is about a girl who was told by a couple of foolish schoolboys that her body did not measure up. This first fall of the soul caught her off guard and, because she did not know what to do, she hid. The girl was a tender age and somewhat innocent to the adversary who "*...prowls around like a roaring lion, seeking someone to devour*" (1 Peter 5:8). Being deceived, injured, and ashamed of her wounds, she took on the burdensome responsibility of saving herself through her own means of control, avoidance, and doubt. These became the loincloths of her soul, referred to as veils in this book, that she would hide behind. It would not be until this girl engaged in a celestial wrestling match with her physical body that the veils could be displaced. In her moment of greatest weakness, this girl would be given an immeasurable gift—a glimpse of the healing power of grace being extended to her through nail-scarred hands.

I would be remiss not to mention how difficult this story was for me to write. And I know, at times, it may be difficult to read, especially if it snags the seams of your own hand-sewn veils along the way. My heartfelt plea for the health of your soul is this—don't ignore the gentle nudge of Christ. He is not scared or ashamed of your brokenness like you are. Heed unto your hearts my story of hiding and muster up the courage to look up boldly from wherever it is you may have fallen. God has already sent His Son to tear the veil that separated our wounding from His grace. All that's left for you to do is open your hands and let the healing balm of His forgiveness and love close your wounds, forever shut.

Chapter Three

the girl in the mirror

I stare forward, she stares back:
A girl I do not know,
one whose silent sufferings
have enabled the lies to flow.

Pulsating within a firm belief
that thinness is a prize,
and once its won, I wear it
like wool over everyone's eyes.

I starve myself to drown the fear
of losing all control.
Yet denying any rightly thing
shall cease to save my soul.

I TIPTOE DOWN THE STAIRS, FEET SINKING INTO THE PLUSH CARPET, TO THE basement of my parents' house. After a brief moment spent groping for the light switch at the base of the stairs, my fingers find the toggle and flick the light on. In the instant it takes my vision to adjust, I feel transported—inside my body while experiencing my past.

Even though this house is different than the one in which I grew up, when I stop to behold all that's around me, I quickly recognize the souvenirs of my idealistic childhood. There's the doll bed in the corner that cradles my favourite blonde-haired baby, Suzy. Her hair is noticeably dishevelled now and the clothes she once proudly displayed have been replaced by an infant sleeper that droops down low, well past her chubby limbs. Next to the cradle stands the play kitchen, crafted by my mother's father when she was just a little girl. It stands stoically as a memorial, holding within its sturdy structure juxtaposing emotions. On one hand, it serves as a sobering reminder of my grandfather's tragic and premature death at the age of fifty-eight. Yet, on the other hand, the soft pink of the kitchen exudes the warmth of his love, still very much alive in my mother's heart. Across from the kitchen sits a small wooden table with two chairs. I fondly remember the tea parties in which I forced my daddy to take a break from his labouring long enough to sit with me. In those precious moments, our love took on liquid form. We drank it in through those tiny cups.

The perfect placement of these toys reflects everything my parents stood for—a life lived with great intention. Their careful thought and consideration exempt no decision, and now these carefully-positioned toys delight the grandchildren each time they visit.

I find the object I've been searching for: the tall oak cabinet tucked away purposefully behind the stairs. I carefully scan the rows of brown photo albums, each exquisitely inscribed with the corresponding year of memories it holds.

According to my mother's Grade Four teacher, she had "absolutely perfect penmanship," a genetic disposition that certainly skipped over my own DNA. Even though I am a certified teacher myself, I have always struggled in this regard. Writing neatly takes concentrated effort, almost exhaustingly so.

I brush the outline of the perfectly-formed numbers with my index finger, remembering how my mother labelled every single one of my pencil crayons with her flawless lettering. My mother cared deeply for order; it was one of the many languages of her love.

As I scan each album, the soft pads of my fingers are pricked by a few years: 1986, the year of my birth; 1991, my first day of kindergarten; 1992, the year my parents scrimped and saved every last penny so that they could take us all to Disney World; 1994... I pause as a familiar wave of shame washes over me. I reach for the smooth leather skin, and my hands begin to tremble, for its contents hold a secret I can hardly bear. I grasp the album and dive straight into the memory it contains.

Staring fear square in the face can be extremely daunting due to the element of surprise. We fear what we do not know; we fear the unexpected. I think this is especially true when it comes to our own ripped skin, our torn apart souls. It is easier to quickly bandage the wound, hiding it from view, than expose it to further inspection. What if poking and prodding inflicts more pain than I can manage? What if the wound bores down deeper into my being than I thought? What if recovery requires me to embrace this change, rather than follow my instinct to run from it?

My mind thumbs through my own personal anthology, where numerous stories have been bound in order that they may be retrieved and retold. Certainly, this is what God had in mind with the Bible, yet, in knowing our bend towards doubt, He ensured His stories could be perceived with more than one of our five senses. All sixty-six books that make up the Bible have helped me understand the grand rescue narrative God has been writing since the beginning of time. When the different genres of the Bible are viewed in isolation, like hearing only the separate parts of a chorus, they can seem oddly disjointed. However, when these parts of God's song of redemption are sung together in perfect harmony, it is nothing short of a masterpiece. It is a song heralding good tidings for those with aching bodies and wounded souls.

In the same way that God designed our skin to produce their own Band-Aids, he fashioned the Word to be tenderly applied to the wounds of our souls. Over time, with repetition that gives way to belief, the wound closes in.

As I ruminate on my choice to dive into my fear, I can't help but see myself joining hands with Moses, the son of a humble Israelite couple, whom God chose to lead His people out of the bondage of Egyptian slavery.

Moses feared.

Moses knew he was ill-equipped for the job.

His tongue was not eloquent in speech and he lacked leadership confidence (Exodus 4:10). Yet God chose him still, perhaps because Moses *was aware* of his inadequacy and did not try to refute it. Interestingly enough, God is the first one to assure Moses that he was created exactly how He intended: "*Then the Lord said to him, 'Who has made man's mouth? Who makes him mute, or deaf, or seeing, or blind? Is it not I, the Lord?'*" (Exodus 4:11).

God purposely created Moses, deficient as he may seem in his own eyes, to display God's great strength. Humility makes a way for the supernatural. In fact, it necessitates it.

While I don't set out to part the Red Sea or lead a nation through the desert, I concede, as Moses finally did, to God's plan. I take the first step toward uncovering the truth about myself, however painful it might be.

I exhale and open the brown album. It feels heavy. I lay it down on the floor in front of me as my eyes rest on the first picture taken in January of that year. I smile at the glowing eight-year-old girl proudly donning her winter snowsuit as she sits on a jet-black GT racer beside her older freckle-faced brother. The girl looks strong, unafraid, and whole. I remember that girl—after all I was her, though I no longer am. I can't trace the road to get back to her although I know the journey forward all too well.

Spring came quickly in my Grade Three year and our teacher, Ms. Cotton, was all too eager to let her oxygen-starved students breathe the budding spring air, and so she took our class on a walking field trip around the community one early April day.

"Quickly kids, pick a partner and line up," she announced in a hurried voice.

Why are teachers always so frantic with their instructions? I contemplate this as a teacher myself, and I'm left puzzled and amused at the same time. Perhaps it's because control is elusive, constantly out of our reach, and yet desired all the same.

My friend Abbi scooted in next to me, and I breathed a sigh of relief. It seemed everyone's entire self-worth in Grade Three depended on two factors: having someone to play with at recess and not being the last one standing after partners were summoned.

"Okay students, where are your bags? When you come across litter, I want you to pick it up and place in it your bag. Our job is to beautify our community. Afterwards, we are going to talk about ways we can raise awareness in our community about littering," Ms. Cotton chirped across the forming line.

Abbi turned and gave me a jab in the side. I was starring at the blue sky, envisioning the approaching summer and all the camping my family was planning to do. Captivated by my daydream, I hadn't noticed the line had begun to move.

"Come on, Kerri, you're holding up the line," shouted Brent, a fiery red-head in line behind us.

I abruptly abandoned my thoughts and started forward, clenching my aching side. Catching a glimpse of a pop can out of the corner of my eye a few meters ahead, I lunged forward to grab it. Behind me a snicker broke out in the same way air might escape a sealed container. Without even looking, I knew the outburst was at my expense; a familiar heat began to climb its way up my neck and spread across my freckled cheeks as I found my place back in line. Abbi turned behind me to face Brent and his friend Kevin, who were gesturing wildly with their hands. I turned.

To this day I wish I hadn't. I wish I kept my eyes forward and ignored their schoolboy foolishness. Unfortunately, my curiosity was piqued, and I had to know why they were laughing. I *had* to.

Brent looked me straight in the eye. I know this because I distinctly remember the red from his hair setting his pale blue eyes on fire, a fire that leapt to his hands as they pointed vulgarly to my backside.

"Did you pack pillows for the walk too?" he sneered, which sent Kevin back into a fit of laughter.

Abbi looked away, but not before I caught a faint outline of a smile part her lips as she stifled her own laughter.

The lightning crack to my young soul was quick and sharp, and the thunder that followed, deafening. *Fat, ugly, stupid, worthless*—I could hear nothing beyond these rumbles. I was the girl on the bike once more, falling with no warning and no time to prepare.

Before this encounter, I had never ever, not even once, thought of myself as fat. To everyone around me, including myself, I was an active (slim, even) average girl. Not too tall, not too short, just a Goldilocks-sized chair that felt "just right" in her own skin.

That is, until *then*.

Untended hurt always manifests more hurt. Compacted emotions mount in pressure, eventually splitting earth and spewing forth emotional debris. I know this now, but I did not back then.

I reach, with heavy arms, up to the oak shelf and slide out the album labelled 1997 in my mother's signature script. The hinges of the album creak upon opening, mirroring my own soul's reluctance to being exposed. I slide a picture out of its hiding place, and my body slinks back against the cool air-conditioned walls. I stare at the picture long and hard. It is a picture of me at camp, the summer after Grade Six ended. I am crouched down on one knee, petting a miniature pony. A tear cascades down my face and lands on the photo. It soaks through the paper, right where the photo shows the hinge of my knee protruding out of my leg like a foreign object—my flesh noticeably shrunken away and hallow. Swallowing hard, I trace the outline of my frail body up to my eyes. They are disproportionate to the rest of my face, as if someone took a straw and sucked hard at my cheeks. I breathe deeply, willing my body to relax.

There's a moment in Exodus, sometime after God rescues Moses and the Israelites from slavery, and then again from the hand of pharaoh and his troops by parting the seas, when God descends on Mt. Sinai in a flurry of thunder and fire. He intends to renew His covenant with Abraham, Issac, and Jacob, with His exiled people. The mountain is literally burning by the mere presence of the holy God, and in the midst of all the thunder, lightning, and roaring flames, God calls Moses up to speak to him. Moses should be absolutely terrified, however the biblical account simply states, "*...And the Lord called Moses to the top of the mountain, and Moses went up*" (Exodus 19:20).

He went up.

No hesitation.

No questioning God.

No bartering for a more convenient location.

Moses simply obeys God's instructions despite the potential dangers that await him. The only explanation I can muster for this unconditional obedience is that Moses must have feared God so greatly that it overpowered his fear of practically everything else. I cannot think of too many experiences more frightening than climbing 7000 feet up a burning mountain. Although it is not stated, I believe we can infer that, to Moses, disobeying God's call was not an option, no matter how scared he might have been. His actions speak volumes. If we fear God more than anything else, we also set ourselves up to trust God more than anyone or anything else.

For far too long, I kept the story behind the photo hidden because I was afraid that, if I were to peer inside the cracked soul behind those fragile eyes, I would not reconcile with what I found. I feared the broken shards of my soul would begin to tear away at the life I so desperately wanted and render it utterly worthless. I simply did not fear God enough to fully trust Him to work *all* things for good (Romans 8:28), even the things I'd rather keep hidden. I was blind to His plans to repurpose my pain. But, as Moses greatly exemplified through his unshakable confidence, fear—if we let it—only prevents us from experiencing God's transforming grace. The very reason God called Moses up to the mountain was to invite *His* stubborn and deeply rebellious, doubting people back into a covenant relationship founded upon trust and grace: "*The Lord passed before Moses and proclaimed, 'The Lord, the Lord, a God merciful and gracious, slow to anger and abounding in steadfast love and faithfulness, keeping steadfast love for thousands, forgiving iniquity and transgressions and sin…*'" (Exodus 34:6–7). Moses feared God more than anything else and trusted God more than anyone else because he knew the character of God more than anybody else.

I allowed Brent's words to echo off the walls inside my mind, uttering not a word to anyone about the injury I had sustained. Like an unwelcome grass that springs up between paving stones, shame began to grow amid the cracks of my soul. It altered the way I saw myself, distorting the image before it was reflected back. When you look at a distorted image of yourself long enough, it becomes the only image you are able to see.

Even though there was nothing wrong with my body, over time I began to think I must be overweight. It was a lie that lurked about my day as consistent and dark as my own shadow. Tired of the inevitability, I believed this thought held for me a life of being unwanted—and bombarded with images of desirable people, at the tender age of ten, I took matters into my own hands.

The only person on the entire earth to whom I have exposed this particular soul wound at the time of this writing is my husband—for we learned long ago the danger that lurks in secrets kept and have made every effort to build our relationship on deep piles of concrete trust. Timothy Keller speaks of two features of real friendship, which my husband and I have found inexplicably true—constancy and transparency. In his book, *The Meaning of Marriage*, Keller goes on to quote Dinah Maria Mulock Craik, a writer who describes a relationship that perfectly marries these two characteristics:

> ...the inexpressible comfort of feeling *safe* with a person—having neither to weigh thoughts nor measure words, but pouring them all right out, just as they are, chaff and grain together, certain that a faithful hand will take and sift them, keep what is worth keeping, and then with the breath of kindness blow the rest away.[4]

It was almost ten years into our marriage before I finally conceded to let my husband sift through my story. I had recently attended a women's conference in Minneapolis where I clearly heard from God a call to write. I knew then that writers must consent, in one way or another, to live transparent lives. Therefore, upon returning home I mustered enough courage to show him my youthful attempt at re-sowing my own soul flesh. He was my Thomas, and I was fumbling my way toward Christ by letting him brush his fingers across my scars.

Even though I was confident in his ability to be trusted, and sure that a fountain of kindness would spring forth from his heart, that disclosure took monumental strength and supernatural bravery. Through it all, I learned a most valuable lesson: Secrets never protect you, they persecute you. Secrets hole you up in a prison cell, demanding a ransom you will never be able to pay. Secrets trick you into thinking there's a lock on the cell door, when the mobilizing truth is that Christ died to set us all free (John 8:32). He is waiting on the other side of that thing you think you cannot face—that thing that's got you weary and needing rest—with a yoke that is easy and a burden that is light (Matthew 11:30). Christ wants to redeem the very secrets of which you are most ashamed. Trusting your whole story to God is like putting good seed into the hands of a capable and generous sower. One day you just might awaken to a plentiful harvest of the most beautifully ripened fruit grown from the fertile ashes of your sorrows.

I still remember the tears of compassion that welled up in my husband's eyes as I choked out a river of imperfect words that momentarily lifted the veil. It was a holy moment, one in which the prison doors were knocked down and chains were broken by God's victorious truth alive in me.

Although I was only eight when I first heard the evil lie that every girl hears at some point in her life—that her body is hopelessly flawed—it took until my eleventh birthday for this whisper to crescendo into an audible shout that could no longer be ignored.

Back then, tradition in our household bestowed the birthday boy or girl the honour of selecting what we would all eat for supper that evening. I remember the meal I chose like it was yesterday: store bought chicken burgers, white buns, McCain curly fries breaded and fried with a delicious and kidney-debilitating seasoning salt, and to top it all off a Dairy Queen ice cream cake. It was pure kid salt-and-sugar heaven. Yet, as I stared down at this plate of innocent blessings, hurt and shame began to bubble up from my unhealed wound. When Brent's words first cracked my soul wide open, I was too young and inexperienced at life to know I was not designed to bear the weight of these lies on my own strength.

Like bridges, we are all constructed with capacities. When we are first born, our capacities to handle stress are almost nonexistent; we require our mom's reassuring care incessantly. As we grow, our capacities are determined by our "properties" or the character we've developed. Interestingly enough, according to transport Canada, "the load capacity of bridges is intended to be the safe load capacity, not the ultimate or maximum load capacity."[5] In other words, bridges have rules in place to prevent them from ever reaching their actual limits. Isn't this exactly what Paul envisioned when he wrote to the church in Galatia, "*Bear one another's burdens and so fulfill the law of Christ*" (Galatians 6:2)?

We need a group of people with whom we can trust the hard stuff, all our gut-wrenching, soul-splitting, flesh-rotting wounds—because if the burden is yoked to another trusted soul, we will never be in danger of approaching our maximum capacity.

Unfortunately for me, I was only about twenty minutes past my eleventh year on earth and I didn't have the faintest idea about loads or capacities, nor did I sense the impending reality that my bridge was about to snap. With the faces of the people I loved most staring back at me, I began to feel a sense of urgency to fix what had obviously gone terribly wrong with me. My body and the image that shone back at me in the mirror was the problem, not the words manifested by another's own deceitful heart. If I were more beautiful, skinnier, then I would never have to hear those razor blade words again.

I was in dire need of a receptive ear, someone who could listen to my story and chart my coordinates. I did not realize, at the time, just how far I'd been blown off course. This somewhat typical pre-teen situation had blown like gale force winds against my sails. I was lost at sea. Worst of all, amidst the chaos, I had allowed an immature boy's thoughtless words to become my compass.

With the faint echo of "Happy Birthday" fading in the background, something profoundly deep and dark donned on me. Though it felt wrong, it was strangely comforting. I suddenly, and perhaps subconsciously, became attuned to the fact that what I was experiencing was the inability to control what others said or did to me. I had been blissfully riding along in life, when something tugged my handlebars hard to the left. The only thing I knew to do was to counter this force by pulling right with all my might. I could not control what others said or did, but I could control myself. The same power and autonomy that chose this delectable birthday meal could also choose not to eat it and no one—not Brent, not my parents, not even my own better reason—could stop me. This thought exhilarated me with a freedom and power I had not felt before.

Isn't that how sin always begins, with a rush of autonomy? Taking control of our lives feels powerful, even if it is only an illusion of power at best. We forget that there is a king of the dark in the same way there is a Prince of Peace. All sin can trace its heavy chains back to the one who woos us away from our first love, promising excitement, passion, and independence, only to leave us as abandoned, forlorn adulterers.

John Piper argues that no human being can see the glory of God without His help: "This is not because we are helpless victims of blindness but because we are lovers of blindness."[6] We crave control, and we will often put on whatever blindfold is necessary to attain the illusion of it.

Lights dim with candles swaying softly between me and everyone I held most dear, I slid my hand across the table and pulled the adversary closer to my ear, giving permission for his lies to speak louder than God's truth. I wanted desperately to be loved, desired, adored; I wanted everything that an affair promises a woman who is tired of the old and is being offered something new.

I blew hard at the candles in front of me, the rush of air exiting my lungs just enough to extinguish the last bit of hope that remained. With smoke billowing up in the air, I squeezed my eyes shut and let the adversary's tidal wave of lies break and wash over me.

Chapter Four

the veil of control

Fists clenched, eyes closed,
barricaded behind the veil.
No human word can illuminate
the darkness lurking there.

I hold the steering wheel tightly
in the vehicle that drives my life.
I believe my white-knuckled grip
will steer me away from strife.

I'm struck behind without warning,
some veil obstructing my view.
This collision has rendered me broken—
yet only from wreckage can He build something new.

According to the National Institute of Mental Health, eating disorders are "*...serious and often fatal illnesses that are associated with severe disturbances in people's eating behaviors...*"[7] We need only look to the few first few pages of the Bible to corroborate this definition. Genesis 3:1 opens with, "*Now the serpent was the shrewdest of all the creatures the Lord God had made...*" (NLT).

Stop right there.

Why did God make the serpent in the first place?

What was the benefit of this created evil?

If we were made to bring God glory, surely this serpent was an oversight, a momentary lapse in judgment of our good God?

Perhaps the existence of the serpent so early on in the story reveals a crucial aspect of our existence: free will. God created humans with the ability to choose, even though He knew it would mean we would choose badly.

Jesus reaffirmed faith as a decision when He came to earth and invited the disciples to follow Him. Yes, invites. The creator of the universe, the One who holds the earth in his hands, the One who could easily demand allegiance from every created being, instead, invites us to *choose* Him.

The serpent provided all of humanity with the glorious opportunity to choose. In *The Great Divorce*, C.S. Lewis says this of choice: "There are only two kinds of people in the end: those who say to God, 'Thy will be done,' and those to whom God says, in the end, 'Thy will be done.'"[8]

We may be tempted to believe that the powers opposing God are equal to Him. Although the Bible adeptly warns of the power of sin, it quickly dismisses the notion that evil stands a chance of defeating God because of what Christ is sent to accomplish. The author of Hebrews says, "*...that through death he might destroy the one who has power of death, that is, the devil, and deliver all those who through fear of death were subject to lifelong slavery*" (2:14–15).

We can be encouraged that scripture continually portrays the adversary as helplessly short-sighted and single-minded. He has one prerogative borne out of his own deluded doubt: to create opposition. He chose to live apart from God, and he has been tempting humankind to do the same from the beginning of our time.

I like to imagine all of creation holding their breath as they wait to see Eve's choice. The serpent, dangling selfish ambition before her eyes, deceives her into grabbing the tantalizing fruit, and Eve's teeth pierce apple skin. The metaphor we can mine from the image of Eve biting through apple flesh is astounding, revealing the Great Author's attention to detail.

All fruit has a protective outer layer—the peel. Humans have skin. Our souls have a spirit. The peel protects the fruit from rotting. Our skin protects our bodies from disease. Our spirit, when joined with the Holy Spirit, filters out lies and allows God's truth to permeate through.

In the same way that Eve's teeth pierce the apple's flesh, the serpent's lie tears through her, wounding the only everlasting part of her being—her soul. Once we are exposed and our soul compromised, we become susceptible to illness and sin's devastating effects.

Eating disorders begin with one swift bite through soul flesh. Maybe your story is like mine? Maybe you can remember the words that tore like teeth, leaving a deep wound. Perhaps you didn't know, at first, that, if left untreated, this wound would become a breeding ground for shame and sin to grow and multiply like bacteria. Others who struggle with eating disorders may not be able to articulate when or how their struggle first began. It would seem, however, if we were able to locate the puncture wound, the dental imprint would bear the unmistakable teeth marks of the crafty, little, evil serpent.

Without even glancing at the clock, I know it is 6:00 a.m. by the morning light streaming through the small opening between the bottom of the blind and the window ledge. Much like my hard-working father, I am an early riser. In an effort to combat the incessant urge my body seems to have to awaken near dawn, my parents bought me an expensive blackout blind when I was eight—the kind that are thick with layers upon layers of opaque plastic and a stop pull mechanism that never quite seals the gap no matter what angle you tug. I roll to my side and away from the light, but I can still feel it hot on my eleven-and-a-half-year-old back like a laser searching for the tumour of shame metastasizing in me. You can have a heart full of darkness, yet all it takes is a crack for the light to penetrate and illuminate every hallowed corner where pain pulses. Not me, I decide, not today. I keep my back turned and the light out.

I rub my temples to try to ease the tension already mounting when I consider the series of decisions I must make in order to stay true to my selfish pact. My thoughts are suddenly interrupted by the growling howls of my stomach as it pleads for food. I close my eyes and will for more sleep to relieve me from the agony of living this way. It's hard not to hate what I have become. My digital clock forms the next chunky digit above my head, and I give in to the growling. As I drag my body to an upright position, I can't stop myself from the little ritual that's now become habit. I suck in my breath and look down at my hipbones, which protrude like gnarled horns. For is the devil not always present in our self-loathing? Before I let the air go, I picture myself just a little thinner. I'm chasing a moving target.

I'm now thirty-two, more than two decades past this dark time in my life, and yet I find myself mustering every bit of courage and strength to write these words. You can leave something hidden for so long and bury it so deep that, when you finally shed light on your brokenness and begin the painful process of digging it back up, a well of emotion springs up alongside it.

Katherine Wolf speaks about the power of openness and vulnerability in her book *Hope Heals,* in which she recounts the painful emotions surrounding the aftermath of her stroke, which left her unable to walk, eat, or take care of her young son. She says, "I don't think any of us can tell our most vulnerable stories in the moments they occur for fear that they may undo us. We have to wait until we are in a season of safety before we can open up our deepest wounds."[9]

Slowly, I tiptoe down the hall to the kitchen. The light from the window dances on the kitchen table, almost teasing me with the thought of a joyful feast under this canopy of conspicuous light. I wrap my fingers around the gold cupboard handles and pull the doors wide open, revealing a vast array of cereals, oatmeal, crackers, and pop tarts. Carefully and intentionally, I pick up one box and then another, instinctively flipping each one over to clearly read the nutritional chart stamped to each side. Like a predator hunting for its prey, I focus in on the one piece of information that feeds my unhealthy obsession: the fat content.

These labels were designed to help people decipher whether or not they are making a healthy food choice. For me, these labels fuel my addictive fire by further propelling my need to measure and control every single bite. In writing that's as red as the blood draining from my wounded soul, I read, "Blueberry Pop-Tarts, 0g." Instant satisfaction bubbles up through my cracks. I reach into the package and remove a single Pop-Tart, separating it from its twin. My stomach roars in hunger at the sight of food, forcing me to spar against my fear. I have to eat, I know I do, but why is it so hard? Why can't I just shake this feeling of self-disgust at the sight of myself in the mirror? Why do my thighs feel hopelessly huge and my confidence despairingly small? After I have placed the Pop-Tart on a glass plate, I make haste for the basement stairs. Not one of my other four family members has made a sound this morning, and I am eager to escape the exposing light of the kitchen to eat my Pop-Tart hidden in the basement where the truth cannot find its way through the seams of my busted soul.

As an adult now reflecting upon that time, I find myself asking: What was my greatest fear? Was it looking down upon the body I had become to loath and seeing the inch of fat I could pinch between my fingers? Or was it the fear of being found out, or worse, exposed? Exposing my wounds would require me to re-tell, and in essence, re-live, the wounding—something I had quietly resolved I would never do.

The necessary evil involved in veiling my wounds was losing sight of them myself. After a while, I don't even think I fully understood why I was restricting myself from food—I had become numb to the dysfunction a wounded soul can beseech. In a concerted effort to protect myself from further wounding, my twisted actions simply became normal to me: eating in secret so that no one would see how little I really ate; constantly climbing on and off the bathroom scale; obsessing over every gram of fat that entered my body. Each action was a desperate attempt to determine my own outcomes. I may not have been able to control who or what had hurt me, but I could control this—I became altogether too good at controlling *this*.

One Sunday at church, a long-time neighbour approached my paper-thin twelve-year-old body and ever so gently touched my shoulder with a look of serious concern clouding her eyes. I'll never forget the shock that thundered through my body the moment her fingers contacted my skin. For in the soul of every sister in Christ, the power of Jesus resides and aches to intercede.

Mother Teresa infamously said, "Not all of us can do great things. But we can do small things with great love." Jesus himself was a man who demonstrated the importance of small things done in the name of great love. Yes, He drew crowds and spoke to the masses and rebuked demons. But he also withdrew to have quiet one-on-one conversation with people whose souls had been splintered by the hurt of this broken world.

"Kerri, are you okay?" Her words, though sharp with the truth of the light, still seemed unable to penetrate the thick layers I'd wrapped tight. She pressed on, undeterred, as if she had left her own body and let God in. Is that not entirely impossible? Perhaps God is much more visceral than we ever allow him to be.

"Kerri, have you been sick? You seem so..." Her voice trailed off, and, with it, a thousand possibilities for my condition remained—

Wounded.

Desperate.

Hollow.

I turned away, but not before the sword of Christ's truth, brandished by another's mere proximity and concern, caught the seam of my veil and tugged hard. For a moment the veil lifted, leaving my wounds exposed. The fresh air rushed in, bringing welcome relief to my soul's fiery infection. I suddenly wanted nothing more than to be free of all the layers of control that kept my wounds barricaded from all life-giving oxygen and light. The daily trial of burying my shame while simultaneously holding my head high was becoming difficult to navigate. I longed for someone or something to stop the veil from falling back into place. I sensed a divine possibility of being known and still loved, however, I wrestled myself free from such thoughts before they could win. I was too afraid of the costs associated with disclosure. What would people think of me?

I spread the largest smile I can muster across my lips and turn back towards my neighbour; the subtle movement shakes her hand free.

"Oh," I laugh nervously to drown out the symphony of emotions going on inside. "I'm... fine."

I make haste for the washroom and leave her standing there utterly unconvinced. As soon as the lock snaps shut, I collapse on the toilet seat, gasping for air and fumbling for the familiarity of control I had clung to this past year.

I rest my head against the cool metal wall of the bathroom stall and try to organize the thoughts spinning through my mind. It felt good to decide what went into my body. It felt good to set a goal of losing weight and succeed. It felt good to be skinnier than other girls my age, except for the fact that my soul still burned with the insatiable desire of it all not quite being enough.

In John 4, a Samaritan woman journeys to the community well in the heat of the afternoon at a time most people sought refuge from the blazing sun. Perhaps it is because she secretly hoped she could draw water in peace, far removed from the disapproving glares of the pious Jewish population. You see, much like me, this woman has wounds that bore deep into soul flesh. Something inside of her aches for a deep, soul-satisfying love, but she seems unable to find it despite her numerous illicit romantic relationships. This wounded woman, no doubt exhausted from travel and the weight of the burden she carried, approaches the well and, to her surprise, finds a Jewish man already present. The man is Jesus. Alarm bells probably sound when this man abandons all cultural norms and speaks to her. During this time in history, men were not allowed to address a woman without her husband present. To further compound the absurdity of this moment, Jews and Samaritans were greatly opposed and rarely spoke to one another.

Knowing that the woman hasn't the faintest idea who He is, Jesus simply asks her for a drink of water. She is aghast and undoubtedly feels the need to educate Jesus on the ridiculous nature of his request, so she replies, "*…How is it that you, a Jew, ask for a drink from me, a woman of Samaria?*" (John 4:9). Jesus calmly answers by telling her that the gift of God, which he possesses, is that of living water. This sends the woman reeling. Who is this man that He provides living water? How is she to retrieve this water when He does not have a vessel to carry it?

I can't help but notice a pattern in the way Jesus communicates with people He is trying to redeem. Time and time again, He asks questions to provoke response that probe beneath the veil. Hebrews 4:12 says, "*For the word of God is living and active, sharper than any two-edge sword, piercing to the division of soul and spirit, of joints and of marrow, and discerning the thoughts and intentions of the heart.*" Since Jesus Christ is the Word become flesh, it makes sense that His words bring to fruition the duality of which the scriptures speak, first by deconstructing lies with His questions, and, second, by erecting hope with His grace.

This wounded woman of Samaria has no vessel to retrieve water for Jesus, but that is precisely what Jesus wants her to see. She is insufficient. He is *sufficient*. What she lacks in earthly love, He can make up for with an eternity of belonging. What she thirsts for, He can quench if she but recognizes her wounds—her deficiency. Jesus' compassion captivates the woman's attention and draws her to Him. We know this by her words, "*...Sir, give me this water so that I will not be thirsty or have to come here to draw water*" (John 4:15).

Grace without truth is like love without commitment; it does not have the power to transform us into something more holy. The painful part of this equation is that truth must always come first. Jesus needed to show her the indisputable teeth marks of sin. And so He said, "*...Go, call your husband, and come here*" (John 4:16).

The woman has no husband. She's jumped from relationship to relationship, desperately trying to veil that first injury to her soul. Little does this wounded woman know that all it takes is one bite—and maybe she wasn't even the one who first chose it. Perhaps her father abandoned her as a child, or a sibling abused her trust, or an uncle who she trusted turned out to be unworthy of that precious gift, or the man to whom she first gave her heart taught her that love is measured with deeds rather than protected with commitment and nurtured with acts of kindness. In the process of the wounding, the concealing, and the weeping, she let five men know the sacred parts of her, each one slamming the door with such force that her soul was left splintered. No, we do not know this woman's backstory just as no one may know yours, but rest assured, God does. And in His knowing, not despite it, He left the majesty of His throne to suffer appalling humiliation and heinous rejection in order that He may offer a drink that would finally end his daughter's unquenchable thirst for love, and ours.

After believing she's been redeemed by God's own son, the woman at the well makes haste for her village to tell everyone about this saviour, Jesus, who saw into the dark crevices of her soul and loved her still. Jesus has washed her wounds in grace and bandaged them with truth, leaving her transformed. The God of the universe, who crafted her intricate heart and then lovingly supervised every broken turn her life seemed to take, came down to earth, not to condemn her, but to seek out and save her. He came to showcase her scars as evidence of a remarkable love story to reach the millions of sisters that would one day find themselves wounded at the well.

How many women out there are trapped in the lie that, if we lose control, we also lose our ability to cope? It is a lie we whisper to ourselves in quiet moments when we allow the fear to settle in. Fear over our children, or our spouse, or our jobs, or our appearance, or our health, or the situation with our friend. As the voice of fear grows louder, the promise uttered from the lips of our creator, that we are fully sufficient in Him, becomes a distant memory. Instead, we seek confidence from outside influences—searching tirelessly for our rank in fitness routines and diets and perfect pictures on Instagram—only to be reminded that we'll always come up short.

God gifted us with a whole tribe of beautifully and fearfully created women with whom to live in community, and yet fear drives us into becoming worshippers of the veil. How many times has jealousy usurped the transforming power of brokenness? Sarah despised Hagar, Rachel envied Leah, and only hardship resulted. If only we feared God and the health of our souls more than we feared man and, consequently, status.

"The fear of man lays a snare…" (Proverbs 29:25) says the wise Solomon. His words have not changed. Still, we find ourselves on the same planet thousands of years later and his holy, inspired, life-saving words have not penetrated the thick veils God tore by crucifying His only Son. If only there was a way to stop all the wanting, striving, and aching for purpose long enough to contemplate how fleeting our physical bodies actually are, yet how everlasting our souls were created to be? Maybe then we might finally be able to admit that our competitive and consuming outward striving is all just a little bit foolish.

Reaching this weight will heal all the hurt I've bottled up inside; buying these clothes will melt away my insecurities; using this lotion will erase those bags of fatigue I lug around each day. We may temporarily fix our bodies by slapping tar all over our cracks, but what becomes of our patched life boats when the water keeps rising and rushing in? If we cannot hope to survive in broken bodies, what makes us so determined to press on despite our severely wounded and wailing souls?

Here I was clinging to the cold metal wall of the washroom stall, straddling my own porcelain well of sorts, and I simply could not acknowledge the mirror held up to my face lovingly by my neighbour. The veil of control I had draped over my wound hadn't healed my affliction and never would. At best, my control was a facade of true power; at worst, it was a barrier that blinded me from the truth trying to redeem me.

Even though my veil had lifted long enough for me to catch a brief glimpse of Jesus' truth that day, I lacked the courage to sever the ties and remove my veil of control. Instead, with a wild wind blowing me east, I returned to my village, silent.

Chapter Five

the antibiotic of time

How do we imply worth,
to a person we truly love?
Do we spend the world's currency?
Or a gesture curated above?

God's greatest act of love
involved leaving His throne.
He offered relationship,
that healing may flow.

He bids us to do likewise—
to give time like its breath,
It might be the saving grace,
that mirrors sacrificial death.

"Come on Kerri—three more laps, you're on pace! You can do this!" My coach's voice bellowed into my eager ears, and I pressed hard into the familiar burn rising in my chest. Feet fiercely clawing at the rubber track, I could feel the intensity mounting with each and every stride. I was five laps into the championship 3000-metre track race, but, more importantly, I was on pace to break the rural provincial record for that distance in my age category. I had been training all year for this precise moment, and I wasn't about to succumb to the pain. I had learned quickly that the best distance athletes were the ones who could endure more pain than their competitors; winning, at times, had less to do with talent and more to do absolute grit and determination. I just so happened to possess both of these crucial elements in spades.

I read an article in *Psychology Today* that stated, "When people feel emotional pain, the same areas of the brain get activated as when people feel physical pain."[10] If one accepts this to be true, then it would seem years of running with a backpack full of shame had done much to train me for this particular sport.

My first recollection of excelling in running occurred in elementary school the day my entire Grade Six class completed the gruelling four-lap endurance test. When the teacher shouted "Go," I distinctly remember the girls in my class sprinting in front of me, leaving me in their dust. Being somewhat conservative by nature, I had started the "race" at a pace I knew to be sustainable, for I had run to and from school numerous times in my early years and did not fear the distance that lay ahead of me. After the first lap, many of the girls began to tire and, one by one, I chased them down. After two laps, I was in the lead, and, by lap three, I had clearly separated myself from the field. The final lap saw me passing half the class, finishing the endurance test exhibiting nothing more than a mild rise in respiration rate.

The following year, after observing me in the school-wide "run-club," my Physical Education teacher signed me up for the junior high zone meet where I ran the 800-metre and 1500-metre, capturing both titles with ease. Three years later, I repeated a similar feat at the high school provincial championships, winning the 1500-metre and 3000-metre, and coming in second to a girl (now lady, who just competed in her second Olympics) in the 800-metre.

Truth-be-known, I was a somewhat cautious kid. My parents enrolled me in gymnastics at a young age, but I never progressed past the intermediate level because I was terrified of a certain gymnastics apparatus known as the vault.

In baseball, I made the travelling team based on my ability to throw and catch the ball, however, once my coaches gave me a bat and witnessed the intense fear I had of the ball hurling towards me, I sat on the bench the rest of the season.

In running, I had finally found a sport where I felt reasonably safe and in control. I was not dependent on others, only on my own mental capacity to hurt and persevere, and I had learned to do that well.

Unbeknownst to me, one hot June day in my Grade Ten year, after I ran my 3000-metre in near record-breaking speed, a man watched me in the crowd and saw in me what still seemed cloudy to my wounded self—raw talent. Our interaction that day set my life on a different trajectory. Although it's been over a decade since I saw Mr. Well's face, his sharp features will forever be etched in my mind. It seems to be that way with people who have a hand in shaping you. The part of them that believed in you can translate over time into tangible belief in yourself. It's a gift they impart, and, if you're fortunate enough, it's permanent.

"You're going to need to do something about that..." Mr. Well said, pointing his aging finger at the long brown pony-tail cascading down my back. His tone was dead serious, yet his eyes were exuding a flicker of joy that was impossible to ignore.

My mother, suddenly noticing a strange old man talking to me, instinctively reached for my shoulders and searched his face for an answer to a question he had not yet asked.

"Your daughter is quite talented, but she could use some coaching. Her hair is too long for one thing, it's making her head bob and her body sway like a sailboat—she's wasting valuable energy. And as for her stride, it's much too long. She needs to learn to move her legs faster; even distance runners have excellent turn-over."

My mother started to open her mouth and then paused. She was intently studying the ruddy contours of Mr. Well's face to see if the answer to a prayer lay hidden somewhere between his unassuming words, an answer that would finally begin to mend her daughter's unspoken brokenness.

Insomuch as the Spirit hovered over the deep, He was there behind the bleachers of the university stadium, when Mr. Well extended his hand out toward my mother. All at once, the dense fog of the past few years lifted, and my mother's faith and sight aligned beautifully.

It took my parents a couple weeks before they dialed the number scribbled on the yellow post-it note kept close by the phone in the kitchen. Mr. Well had offered to coach me that day for no other reason than to help a young girl reach her God-given potential. He would not have put it that way, of course, for he was not the church-going type; he had no time or patience for that nonsense. Regardless of that fact, he had made it perfectly clear to my parents that no monetary fee would be required for his coaching services. He simply wanted to know if I was hard working—to which my parents confidently and enthusiastically replied, "yes."

Given the climate of mistrust in today's society, it is a wonder that my parents were not more cautious when it came to their youngest child and only daughter. The only plausible explanation is that, the moment my mother shook Mr. Well's hand, she was baptized, in the most personal way, with the peace that passes all understanding—a peace that comes after the laborious work of letting go. Thankfully for me, Mr. Well proved himself trustworthy a million times over during the two short years I worked with him.

In our initial months together, our relationship quickly transitioned from new and awkward to familiar and comfortable. He was a stubborn old man who passionately loved running, and I was a stubborn young girl who was looking to love something with equal fervency. As a Physical Education teacher for some thirty odd years before he retired, Mr. Well had seen his fair share of burgeoning athletes in the rural community of Winkler, which was a mere ten-minute drive from the town in which I lived. Now solely focused on coaching track, he had a keen interest in developing raw talent in an effort to "give the city kids a run for their money." He had the motive and I possessed the required talent—therefore, we seemed to be a complementary match.

At the start of our coaching arrangement, we decided that Mr. Well would pick me up from my high school three afternoons a week and drive me to the neighbouring high school so that I could run laps with his other athletes. At first, I was unsure how I would navigate that ten-minute car ride. What would an insecure Grade Ten girl have to say to an opinionated sixty-year-old man that could fill in all the obvious spaces where awkward silence was sure to lurk? It didn't take long for me to figure out that Mr. Well could entertain a squirrel for ten minutes if he must; a shy, mildly intelligent sixteen-year-old in no way intimidated him. On the countless drives buckled next to one another, we worked hard to cross the chasm wedged between us—an old man, slightly jaded by the nonsensical world, and a broken young woman seeking a way out of her brokenness.

On many occasions, the bridge we forged held the weight of us both. I learned the hilarious and sometimes heart-wrenching stories behind his colourful cynicism, and he learned that the world wasn't hopelessly chalked full of entitled youth. Still, infinitely more important than his interest in my talent, or his stories of a life humbly spent serving the next generation of youth, was the message he left firmly pressed upon my heart by sharing something we have all been gifted on this earth—his time. His willingness to give his gift of time to me meant that I must be worthy of receiving that gift, and the ache of worthlessness that I had carried for so long began to subside.

You may never understand how a simple gift of your time can change a life. I had neglected to tell Mr. Well my story, but perhaps—by God's mysterious grace—he knew his own version of it.

On one particular day, while dropping me off at home, he parked on my parents driveway. Our conversation ended naturally, yet a lingering silence seemed to stir something in both of us.

"Kerri?" he asked, without looking directly at me. "What do you eat in the morning for breakfast?"

It was a simple question and, as if it were a test, I knew exactly how to pass.

Without even flinching, I responded, "A piece of toast, a glass of milk. Oh and some fruit," I added for good measure.

When he finally looked at me, I knew he had been granted entry to a door I thought I alone held the keys to. His care and concern for my physical well-being, not only my performance, fostered my own care and concern for my physical well-being that I had not felt for some time.

As I continued to train with him, I learned to appreciate my body for the strong, capable, entity it was, gradually drowning out the echo of the freckle-faced boy's words. I ate things I would not have allowed myself to eat before, such as peanut butter and chocolate milk. Each swallow, free from guilt, brought with it more freedom than the last. Mr. Well's two-year investment into my life proved to me that truth delivered in a vial of quality time is one of the most powerful antibiotics in the world; its ability to fight infections of the soul is often greatly underestimated.

I believe in a God who intervenes in the lives of His people in a variety of ways, whether it be through scripture, dreams, or in this particular circumstance, a person. Although people can be powerful messengers of God's truth, the Bible tells us a story, illustrating that nothing has the power to initiate healing quite like encountering Jesus Christ. The book of Acts describes the life of Saul before he became Paul. Saul was a Jewish persecutor of the early Christians, committing heinous acts against them. He would have been made subject to the truth through many people, and yet he was never completely transformed by it. Not until his face-to-face encounter with the risen Christ did the blinding scales fall from his eyes, allowing him to fully behold the truth and bear witness to it.

I would experience, later on, a personal transformation that would closely mirror Paul's. Thankfully, the antibiotic of time Mr. Well administered gifted me the health to experience such a conversion.

With my lungs burning and one lap to go, I pressed harder into the throbbing pain. Tearing my eyes away, momentarily, from the rhythmic pounding of my yellow track spikes, I glimpsed Mr. Well's stoic expression. He was closely following the digital watch flipped backwards on his wrist, and, through the facade of his serious poise, I caught the familiar flicker of joy his eyes contained. I knew immediately that I was on pace to break the record we were both hoping for. Though I was subjecting myself to excruciating physical strain and every muscle in my body was pleading for forfeit, my mind went to a place for which many athletes search, but few find. A place where I was completely transported outside of my pain. I floated across the finish line effortlessly, right into the arms of my ecstatic coach.

"Well done, you did it, 10:09!" Mr. Well exclaimed, enveloping my small frame in a big hug. Looking up into the crowd, I saw my parents quickly shuffling down the steps of the bleachers to the rubber track. I opened my arms wide to welcome their warm affection. The four of us remained on the track, huddled together in celebration, for some time. None of us seemed to mind the rain that softly started falling.

Hours later, when the gold medal was hung around my neck, I felt the heaviness that accompanied it. Defeating this record was a significant accomplishment, one not exempt from the expectation to do it all over again.

The Bible describes Peter as a someone who whole-heartedly longed after Jesus, yet one who often lacked the endurance to follow through on his convictions, especially early on in his discipleship. One particular night, Peter and a few other disciples were on a boat crossing the sea to Capernaum when, *"The sea became rough because a strong wind was blowing"* (John 6:18). Jesus, knowing his disciples were terrified, walked out onto sea to meet them. But, when they saw Him, they assumed He was a ghost and cried out in fear (Matthew 14:26). Jesus, seeking to comfort his friends in their distress, "*...immediately spoke to them, saying, 'Take heart, it is I. Do not be afraid'*" (Matthew 14:27). And Peter called back to the saviour he desperately loved, saying, *"...Lord if it is you, command me to come on the water" (Matthew 14:28)*. Jesus called for Peter to come and, remarkably, Peter did just that. He jumped out of the boat, eyes fixed on his saviour, and began to walk on water towards Jesus.

If we read no further, this is where we would pause to applaud Peter for his bravery and trust. How many of us have had our own bold and brilliant Peter moments? Perhaps we were deeply moved during a retreat, or time of personal worship, boldly proclaiming, "I am yours God, I will follow you wherever you want me to go." Only, like Peter later on in the story, we open our eyes to the reality of life's capsizing waves and feel our knees buckle beneath us. Receiving that diagnosis, or losing someone we love, or falling into a depression that we fear might swallow us whole, causes us to forget we are held only as long as we believe we are held.

In the weeks following my race, I found myself rowing out to sea. God was setting me on course towards my saviour—towards healing. From the safety of my boat, I could see Jesus off in the distance, coming towards me, and, with great trepidation, I called out His name. He answered back. With wobbling legs, I rose, ready to take those first few steps onto the tumultuous seas. As soon as the icy water slapped against my legs, I looked down. Fear crashed against me, and my instinct was to cling to something I could physically touch—something *I* could accomplish. A different voice called out through the swirling wind, "here is your chance to *prove* your worth." I swallowed the words, salty like the sea, leaving my mouth thirsting for more. Jesus was a mere stone's throw from my reach, and I chose to listen to the howling wind of the adversary instead.

Rather than let go of control and surrender myself to the One whose face I was born remembering, I looked, instead, for a life-saving device—yet another veil—to save myself. I chose accomplishment, the earthly thing within arm's reach, rather than exercising the faith I could only hope for and not touch. Instead of embracing the storm as a means to carry me into open palms of the one true saviour, I cursed it as a means to destroy my better plans.

Chapter Six

The Veil of Avoidance

If it's not acknowledged,
it doesn't exist.
If it doesn't exist,
it is bound to persist.

My high school track accomplishments landed me an athletic scholarship to the University of Manitoba, which promised to pay for my tuition for all five years of my eligibility, with the caveat that I was able to compete. Additional scholarships would gift me the luxury of not worrying about living expenses either. I was swimming in a sea of accomplishment and opportunity, and yet, when I received the gold and brown letter in the mail with the signature bison emblem, my insides churned in apprehension.

I was a girl, like many others, whose soul had taken a tumble. And rather than wrestle with the discomfort of vulnerability, I had chosen to wear the guise of someone who was in control and succeeding at life. I donned this veil in order to protect me from my ever-present anxiety of being "found out" or, worse, falling again. It was as if my full-time occupation was scaling a tightrope between reality and falsity. I was engrossed in the task of staying upright on the wire—the work was mentally and physically exhausting. Even so, off in the distance of my consciousness, my deafened ears could faintly hear the Spirit's words behind them saying, "*...this is the way, walk in it...*" (Isaiah 30:21). God's holy presence still living in me whispered promises of freedom if I could only tear these weighty veils and hold up my soul to the warmth of His light.

But to be freed I had to let myself be known. The parts of me I most wanted to hide out of shame needed to be humbly revealed and tenderly accepted. I had to be shown, by another, how I'd fallen prey to the adversary's lie that I could be made whole by pursuing "*...all the kingdoms in the world and their glory*" (Matthew 4:8). It was the same temptation Jesus faced when the Spirit led him into the desert to be tested. And it was there where He modelled for us how the Word of God *and* trust in a good Father could overpower the adversary's cunning devices.

I had started down a path of accumulating earthly praise without full knowledge of its destination. I had consented to idolatry, unaware that I was being masterfully manipulated by the most sinister of deceivers.

When I showed the letter to my parents and two older brothers, they were ecstatic. They didn't seem to sense my trepidation that lurked beneath the veils I wore. I convinced myself that the only way for me to continue to save face without letting down or letting in those I loved most was to accept the scholarship and begin my university track career.

Mr. Well did not feel like the University of Manitoba boasted the best coaching options for a young woman like myself, but he understood the desire to be close to family (it was a mere hour and a half from my hometown) and, therefore, supported the decision with as much enthusiasm as his better reason could muster.

One day after I arrived in Winnipeg, my new coach sent a veteran athlete to meet me at my apartment for an "easy" run. Not knowing what that meant according to university training standards, I obliged and started out with her. We ran for forty-five minutes at a pace that completely clobbered me. Although I possessed a natural endurance that was next to none, I did not realize that, compared to these seasoned university athletes, I was very untrained. After the run, I took a long shower and went to bed. The next day was my first day of classes as well as my first track "workout" day, and I was already physically and emotionally drained.

I awoke to stiff muscles and a pounding head. How I was going to walk the two kilometres to school, endure a full day of classes, and then work out was beyond me. Thankfully, I shared an apartment with my older brother, and his presence that morning set me at ease. I made it to school, survived my introductory classes, and then waited for 4:30 p.m. to roll around.

The team met at the indoor track called the Max Bell Centre, even though it was outdoor cross country season. I set down my backpack beside one of the girls I recognized from my high school competitions, Lisa. Throughout high school, she jokingly referred to me as "steroid girl" because I always won my races by such a large margin. She smiled when she saw me, and I was happy to sit beside an amicable face. Glancing around the room, I found an older boy who I had seen racing for the Bisons when I was at Max Bell for a competition in my Grade Twelve year. He was surrounded by a group of eclectic, yet serious-looking athletes and seemed to be at the centre of their conversation. It was obvious to me that he was well liked. Our coach, Mark Bernstein, called the meeting to order and introduced the track and field captains to the rest of us. The boy I had noticed turned out to be the male captain. His name was Sam.

My first weeks of training on the track team brought me to the very brink of my capacities. Being stubborn and resilient, undoubtedly due to my mixed Mennonite and Irish heritage, I did not tell my coach that the training was pushing me beyond my limits and better reasoning. I wanted to be accepted on the team and, in order to do that, I felt I had to appear as though this amount of training was normal to me, even though it was more physically demanding than I could have ever imagined. In addition to three two-hour workouts, I was expected to run for forty minutes twice a week and then power through an hour-long run on the weekend. Previously, my training normally consisted of running three to four times a week, rarely for more than twenty to thirty minutes at a time. This new training schedule was an enormous leap, and I should have voiced my concern. My pride, however, silenced the quiet voice inside of me pleading for reprieve.

Compounding the pressures of a new training regime were the adversary's lies convincing me I needed to achieve my worth. Although I was not gripped by an eating disorder with the same intensity as before, I was still wounded—still overly conscious of what I consumed. Due to the fact that many of the girls on the team talked about their weight,

I viewed my slender physique as something I *needed* to maintain. In the world of distance running, a lower body weight usually yielded faster times; weight was one of the few things you could control as an athlete. Having grown accustomed to the veil, I clung to these half-truths and used them as a reason to hold fast to the adversary's lies wooing me away from Christ's truth—that His love for me had achieved far more than I ever could on my own.

One locker room conversation that happened after I'd been on the team only two weeks played over in my mind numerous times that first year. I was changing into my workout clothes and saw that my teammates were *all* slender, muscular young women. None of us needed to lose weight. I cannot accurately say what these young women thought of me so early on in the year, but I do know it bothered them that I trained with the men's coach, as Coach Bernstein decided. Even though I was a rookie, my times were markedly faster than most of the women on the team. There were only two female athletes out of about forty who had a quicker 3000-metre time than me. One of them trained with the men's coach, and the other had recently returned after a five-year hiatus to her women's coach, Eric Watters. It was safe to say that I was a threat to the firmly established veteran hierarchy. Looking back, I don't think I stood the chance of being accepted due to that reality. It also goes without saying that girls can be especially cruel when they want to be. I was no stranger to the evil one could conjure.

One of the women on the team, three years my senior, was pulling on her shorts when she caught the corner of my eye. It seemed to me that, in that brief moment where our eyes exchanged glances, she was granted access to my deep-seated insecurities. Or, perhaps, it was merely that my insecurities about my body were quite commonplace among women.

"I wonder if Coach Watters will put us on all a saltine cracker diet like he did last year?" she said as she smiled wryly, quickly looking away from me and down at her socks.

"He once put me on a diet of saltine crackers for a month," another replied.

"He recommends that to all the girls that need to lose weight," echoed the team captain as she scanned the locker room for worried eyes.

Most women know that fear holds some sort of power, even if it is only short-lived. Women use fear to manipulate, control, or intimidate. In this case, I think their words attempted to serve as a warning siren to all of the rookies, if not only for me in particular. If I thought I was in the slightest way "good enough," I needed to think again. In a fiercely competitive environment such as this, one needed sharp arrows and killer accuracy to beat her opponents. Insecurity regarding body image was an easy target to hit—it rarely missed.

As intended, their siren sound pricked my ears and further cemented my belief that I needed to be thin to win. I could not easily shake off their words or deny their power. This encounter strengthened my resolve to earn acceptance and self-worth through achievement.

Over the next few months, I discovered that I could not make the senior girls on the team like me. This became especially troubling to my naturally unassuming, kind-hearted character, because I had few girlfriends to spend time with on the long weekends away from my friends or family. During my cross-country season that fall, we travelled nearly every weekend to compete. More often than not we travelled by bus, and more often than not I found myself searching for a kind face to sit next to, only to see confident faces bent low, purposefully avoiding my hopeful eyes.

When our son was two, he slept in a bedroom on the main floor next to our living room. As a somewhat rambunctious kid, we set him up with a mattress on the floor to prevent any serious injuries from occurring (we had already made a few trips to the emergency with our fearless son).

Our evening routine at the time consisted of putting our two kids to bed around 8:00 p.m. in the hopes that my husband and I could exchange a few words while relaxing on the couch before collapsing into our own bed for the night. This didn't sit well with our son. Since birth, he had always preferred the physical presence of another over being alone. When he became keenly aware of his family and surroundings at five months old, he began to wake up incessantly during the night unless my husband or I was in the room with him.

By the time he was one, we noticed that, although he could play independently, he never strayed far from us and constantly desired our approval over what he was doing. By two, not much had changed, and going to bed alone was one of his least favourite activities.

On this particular night, my husband and I were exhausted from caring for our sick newborn and managing the ever-increasing behavioural challenges our son seemed to present. We were resting on the couch and could not even muster an ounce of authority to tell our son to settle in his room, despite the grunting and shuffling we could hear echoing off his walls.

About twenty minutes later, I realized the commotion had silenced, which piqued my curiosity. Hoisting my weary body off the couch, with only a mother's relentless love propelling me forward, I turned the corner and caught my breath. My son had dragged his heavy mattress across his room to the threshold of his door and lay there motionless in a heap of stuffed animals, in closest proximity to us that he could possibly achieve without consequence. Gazing at my son's peaceful unassuming face, I was struck with the truth that we all have been wired by a relational triune God to live in community with others. Our insatiable desire for relationship and acceptance should drive us straight into community with our creator, yet we often miss the opportunity to do just that.

Having grown up with two older brothers, I soon gravitated towards the men on the team. They were kind, uncomplicated, and appeared genuinely happy to have me there. At that time, I was still dating my high school boyfriend and so the thought of romantic love was not foremost on my mind. I simply desired a small community where I was accepted and appreciated, and it did not take long before I found exactly that among my male teammates. In a short time, these training partners became like family to me.

On the long bus trips, we would talk, or listen to music, or joke around. I've always loved to laugh. And, in the evenings at the hotel before race day, they always invited me to partake in their movie watching or video gaming, despite my comical James Bond shooting skills. I began to know these people and, although they were not like me in many ways, intentional relationship often fosters love, though people usually believe it is the other way around. During this time, I remained convicted in my faith, or at least the laws on which my faith was built. I can clearly see now that this legalistic resolve, however skewed, saved me from a multitude of sorrows.

The competitive track atmosphere could be toxic, especially once the competitions were over and the infamous after parties ensued. Most of my teammates would drink themselves sick in the hopes of falling into bed with another warm body to ease their lonely hearts for one night. The ache for love and acceptance in this community was palpable. With vision enhanced by the Spirit, I saw through these coping mechanisms to the raw tenderness of their hearts and, strangely, it percolated within me a holy love for these newfound friends.

To this day, I know my parents' countless prayers clothed me with the determination to swim upstream away from the turbulent current which pulled people under. Almost inexplicably, I had no desire to drink or become tangled up with people disillusioned by their life-of-the-party identity.

One night in particular, when I should have been celebrating because I had just secured a coveted spot at the national cross country championships as a rookie, I lay in my bed and silently wrestled with whatever it was that had pulled me under the covers of my hotel bed early. I could not explain the way I loved running and loved these people and yet possessed little desire to conform to their culture. I was in essence excluding myself from further intimacy with my newfound community and not even sure why. This is the mystery of prayer and the power of intercession. The protection guarding my mind and decision making was a heavenly armour placed upon my weak flesh—unbeknownst to me at the time—and I am forever grateful for the many silent heart felt prayers that carried my name up to the heavens.

Even though I had veiled my wounds, first with control and now avoidance, my soul was still accessible. I was hiding, but not hidden. Reflecting on this paradigm as a parent gives me great hope. As Isaiah prophesied, the "rivers of difficulty" will come. The waters may rise up to the heads of my two precious children and, due to physical or relational distance, I may not even know—yet the Bible paints for us a remarkable picture of the Lord not only listening, but bending down, straining His ears to pay attention to what we are saying (Psalm 116:2). All the while, His Spirit roams the earth "*…to give strong support to those whose heart is blameless toward him…*" (2 Chronicles 16:9).

We can know He is faithful when His children forsake Him. We can trust He is fully capable when His children are not. Because He is the Lord our God, the Holy One of Israel, our saviour. And He has promised that even if we abandon our mission on earth or the whole earth abandons us, He *will* be there.

Chapter Seven

the riverbank of faith

The river of life
pursues its course,
widens its mouth,
and increases its force.
A greater volume of water
puts its banks to the test.
Sand will erode—
rock withstands stress.

As it was only eight weeks into my university running career, I felt the first major blow of debilitating injury. I was officially diagnosed with iliotibial band syndrome (ITBS) by the track and field athletic therapist and instructed to spend the next three weeks recovering while cross training on a bike. My body had been enduring weeks of training that it was ill-prepared for, and my poorly-constructed bridge cracked under the weight of its load. Instead of confessing to my coach that every bone in my body ached, not just my ITB, I continued to train with just as much intensity as before. The only difference was that I now measured my progress by the circumference of the puddles of sweat surrounding my stationary bike. This kind of training was most dull, but the fear of losing my edge kept my legs turning those wheels.

The success I experienced on the track fuelled the fire raging within me to achieve self-worth. I became extremely dedicated to my training, rarely missing a workout, despite my body's growing level of exhaustion. I could not be deterred. Each morning, I awoke with eyes fixed on an earthly prize. The error I was beginning to make, however, was not in pursuing running; it was pursuing running with more fervour than I was pursuing God. Quite simply, my loves were falling out of order.

St. Augustine of Hippo, a philosopher from the fourth century[11] renowned for his profound contributions to the faith, first introduced the idea of "disordered loves" in his book, *Confessions*, a deeply personal memoir disclosing his own tendency toward sin. In a more recent translation of this beloved text, Sarah Ruden captures Augustine's words in this light:

> Because of all these things, and other worldly things as well, sin is committed when an unchecked learning toward these, given that they are the lowest order of good things, causes a desertion of the better and the highest, namely you, God our Master, and your truth and your law. These lowest things do have their delights, but not in comparison to you, my God, who made everything. The just person delights in God's self, and God himself is the delight of those with righteous hearts.[12]

My gift of running was a beautiful God-given delight; it was not wrong to find joy in succeeding at it. Rather, I had been deceived into believing running was the *means* by which I could be saved. Unknowingly, I was beginning to exalt a created thing, namely my running talent, above the One who created it in me. And my pursuit of this lower order thing over the highest good—God—is what Augustine argued is the basis for all sin. Although it is certainly possible to exalt God by enjoying a gift he bestows, the gift must be never be sought above the giver. Exalting Him, with or without the gift, is what fulfills my purpose.

Although I could not identify a problem with disordered loves or see how raw my wounds still were, I could sense the pressure to succeed begin to mount. The chaotic waters were rising and the banks of my faith were about to be tested. Over time, however, I became naïve to their susceptibility. Months of believing in a God who should serve my purposes on earth had been depositing sand upon my spiritual banks where I should have been laying down rock.

Jesus, astutely aware of our tendency toward faulty spiritual construction, had this to say:

> *Everyone then who hears these words of mine and does them will be like a wise man who built his house on the rock. And the rains fell, and the floods came, and the winds blew and beat on that house, but it did not fall, because it had been founded on the rock. And everyone who hears these words of mine and does not do them will be like a foolish man who built his house on the sand. And the rain fell, and the floods came, and the winds blew and beat against that house, and it fell, and great was the fall of it.*
>
> —Matthew 7:24–27

Jesus told this parable knowing the storms of life are inevitable. The rain will surely come. The unruly water will rise. And *when* that happens, what I do in the storm matters far less than everything I have done leading up to the storm. By then, the thoughts, beliefs, and ideas I have nurtured about God will become the materials made subject to testing.

After recovering from my injury, I finished my cross-country season successfully by placing in the top twenty on my first national stage. This was a great achievement, one that earned me more scholarship money and the title "rookie of the year" from the western provinces. I was on track for an impressive indoor season, perhaps even a top three spot in the 3000-metre, my specialty, in the country. The discomfort I was experiencing from my wounds, hidden behind veils of control and avoidance, seemed to foment within me a sense of urgency. I utilized every ounce of emotional pain to fuel my training, which yielded much progress.

During the mid-season, we travelled down to Minneapolis to race on their 200-metre indoor track. My body floated weightlessly beneath my legs that day, and I won the race, beating my faster and more experienced teammate in a time of 9:45. That time was the fastest women's 3000-metre time of the year in all of Canada. It was a breakthrough race, one that demonstrated to my coaches and teammates that I possessed the natural talent and drive to succeed that few could achieve.

On the way home from that race, I noticed my right leg felt especially sore. It wasn't the familiar muscular pain that I had lived with constantly during the past six months of intense training; it was a deep ache that did not go away even as I rested on the eight-hour trip home.

I got up early the next morning to meet my training partner for a seventy-minute run. I lived with my brother at the time in an apartment close to university and our parents had graciously lent us a car so that we could easily attend church or drive home on the weekends. My training partner lived across the city from me; I would have to drive to meet her half way. It was Sunday morning, and I knew my brother was planning on going to church with me. Quickly doing the math in my head, I realized I would not be back in time to get us to church by 10:00 a.m. Not wanting to skip this training opportunity, I opened my mouth and let a small lie slide down the tip of my tongue and pollute the air between us.

"I'll be back in time for us to get to church," I said to my brother, who was groggily exiting his bedroom, rubbing his eyes clear to see where I was headed. He searched my face and the moment he met my gaze I tilted my head low. I could not bear the light that spilled forth from his clear sky-blue eyes and the potential it had to illuminate my dark.

"Okay," he said flatly as he walked past me and entered our tiny kitchen.

I could suddenly feel two forces at odds within me. Paul described it this way, "*For the desires of the flesh are against the Spirit, and the desires of the Spirit are against the flesh, for these are opposed to each other, to keep you from doing the things you want to do*" (Galatians 5:17). The sin I had committed by way of my disordered loves was waging war against the Spirit who had not abandoned me. It was I who had allowed His gentle voice to be drown out by my impetuous desire to succeed.

Turning to walk out the door, I cringed as a sharp pain shot through my leg. *I just need to warm it up,* I told myself, hurrying down the hallway to the outside door.

When I finally returned, I glanced down at my watch before turning the gold handle on our apartment door—10:20 a.m. Like Peter when the rooster crowed, I became all too aware of the lie that had departed from my lips mere hours before. It was a blatant sin, and, being deceived, I was quick to shrug it off. I bit into the lie that *my* training mattered more than my brother being on time. Like Eve, my mind foolishly quipped that, if the fruit was ripe and good for eating, what sense did it make to leave it alone?

I readied my defences and stepped into our home to find my brother sitting on the couch facing me. His typically sky blue eyes were unmistakably grey. A thick fog of disappointment quickly filled the room.

"I'm so sorry," I blurted out, attempting to save face. "I completely lost track of time, you can still make it to church!" My words hit the brick wall of his composure and bounced off, his silence halting every possible excuse.

In that moment, I wished he would have struck me with a harsh word to lessen the sting of our newly-fractured relationship, but, in that opportune moment, he wisely chose silence.

Instead, he slowly sat up, walked past me to his bedroom, and firmly shut the door. Tears burned the whites of my eyes as I realized what I had done. I had allowed the adversary's lies of needing to achieve my self-worth play like a soundtrack in my mind until it became the chorus I sang like a crooked tune to someone I dearly loved.

Paul clearly instructs us not to give the adversary a foothold (Ephesians 4:27). A *foothold*, according to the Merriam-Webster Dictionary is "a position usable as a base for further advance."[13] Sin leads us away from being like Christ, advancing the adversary's agenda to discourage and entice us. Just as our bodies continually age and change, our spiritual life cannot be static. We are forever destined to progression or regression, hot faith or cold. For God Himself cautions us against being lukewarm (Revelation 3:16).

That one lie gave birth to many more throughout the following year. I lied to protect my veils of control and avoidance, to keep the breeze of truth from displacing them. I came to believe that the only way to quell the voices urging me to earn my worth was to achieve my way away from them. I did not realize that the foothold I had given the adversary was leading me in a direction that would only cause me more pain. As my branch twisted and curled its gnarled head away from the roots it once grew out of, my actions began to bend towards the character of the one I was advancing towards, and my thoughts began to reflect the voice I heeded. I began to embody selfishness—sinfulness.

After the 2018 Winter Olympics came to a close, I found my heart did not engage in its whirlwind of emotions the way it used to. Although I will always appreciate athletic pursuits and believe that God can fashion great purpose within them, over time I have also come to fear their power to bend people towards selfishness. You simply do not win in athletics with a "you first" mentality.

Imagine four skiers bombing down the mountain in a snow cross event and, as they round the final bend, the leader, looking back over her shoulder and realizing she is going to win the gold medal, purposefully slows down and allows the other three to pass her. Would she then cross the finish line and victoriously celebrate her fourth-place finish? That would be absolutely absurd to the audience, never mind the other competitors!

Athletes are in sport for their own glory, or that of their team, and that's just the way it has to be. Even if you manage to find tangible ways to give back to your sport or encourage your teammates and competitors, the bend towards selfishness in specific areas of your life remains hard to resist.

Jesus, the man who deserves more glory than any other human who skied, ran, or swam across the earth, said in John, "*...If I glorify myself, my glory is nothing. It is my Father who glorifies me*" (8:54). We were created to glorify God, not ourselves. And the most tangible way to do that is through serving with a "you first" mentality. Jesus, the son of God, picked up a serving towel instead of a gold medal and implores us to do likewise. It takes a remarkable person of integrity and strength to pursue one's God-given ability in sport, yet resist selfishness. Those people, such as Eric Liddell, an Olympic miler who refused to bow to the god of sport, breathe fresh air into an environment often stagnant with egotism.

In the rear-view mirror of my life, I see people—like my brother—whom I greatly undervalued under the guise of athletic pursuit, when in reality I was grossly overvaluing myself at their expense. During that selfish period in time, I viewed the needs of others as obstacles that might hinder my progression towards my outward goals, rather than God-ordained opportunities to serve and build up His kingdom—the kind of opportunities that are meant to make up a life.

Jesus' entire life and ministry involved the disciplined practice of being present, of seizing the opportunities presented to Him that He may glorify God. Rarely did He need to go searching, let alone grasping, for glory.

My disordered loves, alongside my resolve to veil my wounds, had placed a barrier between me and the upturned palms of Christ. My fists were tightly clenched. I had not yet learned how to open them up—how to let go.

Wilma Derksen, author of *The Way of Letting Go*, outlines the very personal and profound process involved in forgiving her young daughter's murderer. The idea that resonated with me the most after reading her book was the notion of *letting go* as a posture of the heart that we must choose. Just because it does not come naturally to us does not mean it cannot be learned.

Imagine for a moment a newborn baby bursting onto the scene, lungs wide open to gulp virgin air, yet his tiny wrinkled fists are clenched tight. He remains this way until he learns to open his little hands—learns by being wooed by another. A gentle stroke of his mother's warm hand, a sturdy finger stretched long, ready to uphold his trust, and he soon comes to the realization that the intimacy he craves can be gained by opening up his fists just long enough to grab hold of his mother. In the same way, over time, Christ followers can learn that lessening our grip opens us up to far more possibilities, not less.

At the time, however, I was not ready to trust God with my wounds or my sin. I kept thinking I would find the way to joy through accomplishment. I desired control over my circumstances, foolishly believing God's plan should align with *my* desires. My weakening spiritual foundation necessitated a God who exempted my skies from storms, not One who waded out into chaotic waters with a plan to rescue me.

With fists clenched tight, I greedily plucked fruit from whatever trees would feed my insatiable desire for control. It was the first temptation and the one that lured me back again and again. If only my hands grasped the right fruit, I would know better than God. The irony weaved throughout those first few chapters in Genesis is this: God never intended for us to be groping for more with hungry hands. He designed His garden to produce enough seed-bearing sustenance that none of His children would ever have to steal or starve. We squandered God's abundance and thus gave birth to sin—to loving lesser things.

Loving lesser things may grant us the illusion of control, but, in the end, they become our master, forcing us to strive our way through life with tight fists and hungry eyes. This philosophy is not consistent with God's character. He is, after all, a God of great abundance—the Generous Sower! There is more than enough to go around. It is we who think there is not enough. It is we who think we must gather for today and then tomorrow as well. Little do we know that everything we store up for ourselves—be it accolades, riches, or accomplishments—will only leave us hungry for *more*.

In believing the lie that I knew best, I was, in essence, shunning the words meant to humbly usher me into surrender to the Father's will: *"I know, Lord, that our lives are not our own. We are not able to plan our own course."* (Jeremiah 10:23, NLT). Rejecting this truth drove me to feverishly pluck the fruit that looked best to *me*. In doing so, I was grieving the sure and steady voice, still present in me, whispering, *He has already given you more. Than. Enough.* The Spirit was calling me to freely rest in His abundance, while my flesh was hell-bent on achieving it.

Of all the words St. Augustine penned, there are none that touched humanity so profoundly as when, from the depths of his own sinful despair, he groaned, "our hearts are restless until we find rest in God." There can be no rest apart from loving God first.

I had yet to mine the materials needed, which are made accessible to me by loving God, to stand firm against the rushing waters.

One month after I told that devastating lie to my brother, I stood at the start line of the CanWest 3000-metre finals. What started out as an ache in my leg had grown into a sizable limp. Toeing the line with my fellow competitors, I looked down at the athletic tape wound around my injury in an attempt to give my atrophying leg enough support to race. The tape was given a task it was not designed to uphold. For upon it I placed the weight of an unattainable dream.

The gun fired, and my racing instinct took over. I tucked in behind the girl who had posted times I knew I could beat and focused on my stride. By lap ten of fifteen, I was labouring much more than I should have been. The pain in my leg raged like wild fire. When the final lap bell clanged, I was sweating pain out every pore. Another girl passed me on the final bend, and I crossed the finish line in third place. I collapsed and lay at the end of the rubber track in a heap of sweat and tears. A terrible loneliness closed in on me when I realized the isolation my pursuit of success had cost me—it seemed foolish to call out to a God I'd demoted to second place.

After what felt like an eternity, a firm hand reached out in front of me and kind brown eyes bent low to meet my gaze. It was Sam, the team captain. A reddish hue of embarrassment crept up my cheeks. I grabbed his hand to pull myself back on my feet, but the moment I shifted weight onto my right leg, it buckled and a wave of nausea knocked me flat.

"Woah, easy there" he said, steadying me beneath his arms. His embrace felt familiar, yet it was the first time we had ever touched. My emotions were heightened and wound tight. In an effort to shake my mind clear, I distanced myself as soon as I was upright. Out of the corner of my eye, I saw the athletic therapist rushing over, a look of clouded concern wedged between his brows. Together, they helped me shuffle awkwardly on one leg to the bleachers.

"Are you okay?" Sam asked, trying to make contact with my darting eyes.

I couldn't look up. If I did, the weathered veil might be split in two, baring all my brokenness.

"Sam!" our coach bellowed from the other side of the track. "It's time for the relays." Sam's head snapped up, and in a moment he was gone.

The athletic therapist twisted my leg, and I stifled the urge to howl.

"You need to go for x-rays; it could be a fracture," he stated.

With only a thread of composure holding me upright, I nodded in agreement.

I looked down at my leg and envisioned my perfect season irreversibly breaking, like my bone. Still in mid-thought, my brief brush with Sam's compassion entered my mind without my consent. His unmerited grace had solicited a desire to openly confess to *someone* the ways in which I had not been giving my body the rest or adequate fuel it needed. All at once, I felt flush at the thought of being so intimately known and thoroughly examined. I decided it best to devoid my mind of entertaining such a foolish thought.

Three months later, I stood outside that same brown door of the apartment my brother and I shared. My hand grasped the golden handle, but I couldn't muster the willpower to rotate my wrist. I shifted my weight off the moon boot I wore on my right foot—the one that was fractured in almost as many places as my soul—the one that put a period on my dream—the one that could not hold up under the weight of all my expectations. I stood behind the door of a broken relationship, with a broken foot, still veiling a broken soul, and I had no idea how to begin healing all this brokenness.

When my son was twelve months old, he slipped on a magazine and badly injured his foot. Even though he could not bear any weight on it, he would try to walk every time we put him down, only to find himself, moments later, face down on the floor roaring in pain.

Immaturity beckons us to keep going, keep striving, all while we limp along in our brokenness. It takes someone wiser to scoop us up and tell us how and why we are broken. Perhaps this is what David is getting at when he cries out to the Lord:

> *Search me, O God, and know my heart;*
> *test me and know my thoughts.*
> *Point out anything in me that offends you,*
> *and lead me along the path of everlasting life.*
>
> —Psalm 139:23–24, NLT

David knows he is incapable of identifying his own brokenness. His vision is impossibly clouded and his morality helplessly skewed.

It had been ten long years since I first veiled my broken soul. Ten years of never measuring up, of striving after achievement and acceptance like they were the elixir that would finally bind up every wound and make me whole. In those ten years, I stacked my shelves with athletic trophies, race medals, academic awards, and distinguished titles. Yet they all led me back to the same place—wandering around the garden, howling in hunger, doubting if God had given me enough. Instead of trusting the answer He gave at the very beginning, I tuned my ears to the adversary's voice, believing his lie that I must take matters into my own hand—I must worship a lesser good. This false truth became a defective scab, one that peeled off again and again, always needing to reform rather than transform the wound underneath it.

As I stood behind my door, a new emotion percolated beneath my wounds. It burned with infectious potential—anger. Suddenly, I was alive to this change and the rage that poured out from the foothold that burrowed its way into me.

I opened the door and slammed it behind me. The air around me felt thick like mud. To move forward, I would have to wade through the estuary where these emotions lurked. I so badly wanted to avoid all the mess.

I heard the wheels of my brother's office chair slide backwards in his room and, after a slight hesitation, his door clicked open.

Until this moment, I had never quite grasped the importance of the story in Matthew in which the demons thrown into the pigs "*...rushed down the steep bank into the lake and drowned*" (Luke 8:33). Sin is infectious, but it is also nonsensical and unordered, unlike God. Sin takes away one's ability to see the inevitable; it grasps at any opportunity like it is the only opportunity.

My brother approached me, but what I saw in his place was a mirror reflecting my brokenness. The light streaming through our small apartment windows that day, light that was sent to claim and reclaim me, had, instead, blinded me completely, sending my seething body straight to my knees. With the sin of wild, untamed anger beating inside my chest, I rolled on the floor like an immature child, crying and pounding my fists on the parquet squares. My brother froze halfway down the hallway, unsure whether to approach his shattering sister or trust his engineer instinct to survey the danger first.

I felt words building inside of me, words of hatred over my circumstance and the state of my bodily existence, and they escaped like steam out of the kettle of my soul. The profanities I spewed rose into the air and disappeared, changing nothing yet confirming everything. When I finally looked up, my brother was gone, light through the slit beneath the door the only evidence of his vanished presence.

My fingers fumbled with familiarity for a veil that might protect my consciousness from realizing the full extent of my sin. I needed to grasp something weighty, like a cable knit sweater in the dead of winter, that could press down on all this anger and keep it under wraps. In my haste, I did not take into account the lies necessary to hold each fibre together. The part of me that could touch the veil, and pull it on, and *do something*, was captivated by the feel of its woollen texture and the way the material conformed to me. As I slipped on the heavy veil, I did not see how my soul would be crushed by the weight of these lies: God conducts His business unfairly. God is not good. These lies would ultimately punish me, persecute me, and break me. Because He can never *not* be something He is, just as I will never be *all* that I wish I were.

Rather than open my eyes to receive the light, I shrouded my wounds and shame with a veil more wrought with deception than the others before it—the veil of doubt. Or in Augustine's words, "I made my way farther and farther from you, and you let me."[14]

Chapter Eight

the veil of doubt

Doubt is a blindfold
we wear as a mask
to keep others at a distance
they need not see past.

We wear it with God
to keep Him at bay,
avoiding His sovereignty
to cling to our way.

I OCCUPY THE PASSENGER SEAT OF MY PARENTS' TOYOTA CAMRY AND THE spring sun beats through the window, beckoning my Irish genes to dawn their rosy hue upon my face. My mom awkwardly taps her fingers on the steering wheel, wearing a blank stare as she searches for the confidence to say the words I'm sure she's practised in her head a thousand times.

"Have you been able to make it to church lately?" she finally inquires with a cautionary sideways glance. It is a question that must have been difficult for her to phrase, yet her rehearsed execution comes off so nonchalant it could be mistaken for a comment about the weather or the new pair of royal blue pants she's wearing.

"Oh, church..." My tongue stumbles over the word like I've been awkwardly thrown a football. "It's been... difficult." I force out the words, failing miserably to match her casual tone. It's not a casual topic, though, and we both know it. Regardless, the conversation marches on even with both our defences high.

"The Running Room usually schedules me for work on Sunday mornings," I say. "And then I have to get my long workout in on the bike or in the pool, so there really isn't any time." It's a lie, and I know it even before the words spill out from my lips. I have become numb to the lies I tell to keep the veils pulled taut.

My eyes remain glued on the scenery passing by my window. Although I appear to look at everything, in actuality, I see nothing.

The silence between us continues to place brick upon brick, forming a wall between us and the courage required to be vulnerable. At this rate, the climb might soon become insurmountable.

My mom courageously takes the first step upwards, "Kerri, I think it's important that you try to go to church. You need a community that supports your beliefs." Her words are slow and calculated, like they've been measured with absolute certainty and sanded with wisdom.

Jesus said, "*If anyone has ears to hear, let him hear*" (Mark 4:23) or an iteration of that sentence at least seven times in the scriptures. The son of the Creator knew the intricacies of the ear and the numerous pathways that connect the words we hear to our souls.

The irony of Jesus' statement is that very few of us have no means to receive communication from others. Therefore, the entire phrase hinges on the word *let*. According to the English Oxford Dictionary, *let* means "not prevent or forbid; allow."[15] Although God created our ears, we have great choice in the words we *allow* to flow through them and penetrate our hearts and spirits.

Although painful to endure at the time, the love and truth behind my mother's words was the saline rinse I needed to cleanse my weeping wounds.

Is it not a wonder how we go to such great lengths to avoid pain, as if it only does harm? Birth begins with great pain, yet produces immeasurable joy that cannot be described, only held and beheld.

Perhaps pain is inexplicably tied to the nature of the first sin. Since we desire not to be reminded of being cast out, we run from pain—when in actuality we may be running from the very instrument God is trying to use to reconcile us back to Himself.

"I'm fine mom," I say stiffly. "Quite frankly, I don't feel like I need to go to church to have a relationship with God. I'm really doing fine."

My mom takes a deep breath and chooses silence, her only sound a quiet exhale. Part of me balks at how easily she's disarmed; I almost want to be spurred on, shaken up, poked, and prodded. I want someone else to expose me that I might be saved from the shameful act of disclosing my wounds. This isn't who I was created to be, and it is not who I want to be, yet these veils obscure everything I see and reduce my capacity to respond.

The other day, my husband asked me, "Kerri, if our daughter ever struggles with body image or an eating disorder, what would you say to her?"

That question made me think longer and harder than I should have had to. I am only beginning to understand, as I parent my own children, the position I put my mother in. I know too well the fear of losing a child, whether it be to a physical departure from this earth or an emotional separation. I understand that being present is often wisely chosen over action and should not be viewed as inaction.

Knowing all these things, I hope I would pray relentlessly for the courage to look my daughter deep into her eyes and say, "My daughter, I love you and nothing you do or don't do can change that. I need to ask you some questions now because God has given me the responsibility to tend the garden of your soul. Although weeds may seem insignificant, the longer they are allowed to grow, the deeper their roots burrow. Is there a weed growing in your heart, my dear, that is crowding out God's truth? What is it that you believe about yourself? Are these things wheat or weeds?" Then I would pause, as uncomfortable as it may seem—for the Spirit often requires silence for Him to do His best work.

Allowing God to wrestle us into submissive silence grants Him an open invitation to speak. The problem is we want to know that our struggle into silence will not be in vain. We want to know when He will speak.

After that conversation, praying that my intercession will shed light on a darkened path in some small way, I would envelope her in comfort and love as Jesus taught us to do.

I pray that those would be my words, but I cannot be sure. Although my mother may not have asked me these precise questions, she did do something equally as extraordinary—she drew close and loved me, like

Christ, in my sinful state. With weeds on the very horizon of her view, she gazed upon my garden and saw beauty still.

My mom stops the car outside my apartment and we sit in silence for a brief moment, before her need to ease the tension takes over.

"Can I help you with anything else today, Kerri?" she asks with a sincerity that is equal parts genuine and wholly undeserved.

The Spirit stirring inside of me bids me to claw straight through the veil that's hiding all my hurt and give her a chance to love me—the real me. Nonetheless, the layers feel impossibly stuck, like gauze that's dried to an old wound. Instead, sensing her vulnerability and desperate longing to love me, I pounce on it as an opportunity to gain the upper hand by tugging hard on the yoke we're both bound to by blood.

"I'm fine, Mom, thanks," I say shortly. I get out of the car and close the door, not looking behind me as I walk the twenty metres to my apartment door and turn the key.

Anger is a master manipulator. It can be used as a means to silence another and hold them captive. Anger is also vengeful and desperate and knows no boundaries. It acts out of self-interest and seeks self-preservation. The only antidote to anger is love. The trouble is that there are few things harder to do in life than love an angry person. I still marvel at the way my mother was able to fully and completely love me, despite the hostile anger I exhibited.

Rather than face head-on my pain and confusion regarding God's goodness, I chose to cling to control. By employing the task master of anger to my advantage, I subjected my mother to its cruelty. It's a terrible truth that hurting people will hurt people. Not only does anger manipulate others, it imprisons the angered person nonsensically, like a two-year-old who thinks she is trapped on a merry-go-round and cannot reason that there must be a person who keeps pushing it round, and that person can be told to stop.

Ever since the fall, we have become fearful creatures and often prefer to suffer inside something we know than face the uncertainty of the unknown. Jesus gives us this promise in His word: "*...Resist the devil, and he will flee from you*" (James 4:7). We must muster the courage to bellow a hallowed cry from the depth of our soul that says, "No! In Jesus name, stop this madness!"

The scriptures say we should fear nothing other than God. Even the darkness should not cause us to tremble. After all, we know from God's rhythmic creation that the night is not only predictable, it is necessary on one hemisphere to bring forth the day to the other side. Like all of creation, God invites us to live inside this tension of darkness bringing forth light, pain making way for joy, and death giving birth to new life. When we cut the tension because it is uncomfortable, God's truth becomes partially veiled from our view, and pain and suffering become unbearable. Every force opposing God wants nothing more than for us to feel let down, or even punished. Contrarily, the scriptures proclaim that "*...God so loved the world, that He gave His only son...*" (John 3:16). Isn't this the very hinge on which real love turns? To be loved enough to be sacrificed for. The Bible's greatest love stories, such as Abraham and Isaac, Naomi and Ruth, and finally Jesus, all involve a love that transcends self. For it is this kind of love that propels real change. We can never change outside of being sacrificially loved.

I was loved that way, first by God and then by my dear mother. God was inviting me to peel back the veil that prevented me from fully experiencing the kind of love that first knit my body into being. Nonetheless, I was unwilling to give up control. I *let* my ears be filled with doubt and clung to the veil's false security like a thumb in my infant mouth.

Chapter Nine

the antibiotic of love

Cure the illness,
and find that it comes back.
Cure the person
and nothing will they lack.

Breathing in the warm spring air on a sunny May day, I see hope springing forth through creation in the branches proclaiming the arrival of their leaves. The vibrant green of spring illuminates our previously dull earth for a glorious few weeks each year. Is it not true that spring's precise shade is more alive and sensational than the deep green that settles in with the summer months? Almost as if to say there can be no assurance of warmer weather without first igniting hope.

The aroma of a backyard barbecue fills my nostrils, and I pull myself away from my own swirling thoughts back to my present reality.

"Kerri, are you training again?" asks Mike, a friend from the track team.

"Yea, I'm slowly getting there. I've got a couple of weeks of easy runs under my belt now. It feels good." My words give off an air of assurance. In reality, however, I'm wavering in fear.

"She's probably already ready to whoop you, Mike," jokes Jason, who thrusts his elbow into his friend's side, adding insult to injury.

He looks back at me for approval, something I've become accustomed to over the past nine months on the team. For some reason, he is taken by me, as is evidenced by his many attempts to date me, which have proven largely unsuccessful thus far.

Looking back, I see yet another outstanding example of intercession on my behalf. How many times has a wounded woman fallen onto the path of a man who was not designed to show her the way to wholeness? When we give ourselves solely to the passions of the flesh, we at most obtain a version of happiness, and at worst, experience disappointment or even abuse. What we will never find is lasting pleasure—the free and gracious gift bestowed on those who experience the open arms of the constant, never faltering Father.

As my friends jostle and joke with one another about the upcoming track season, the wafting aroma of chicken draws my attention to Sam, who is standing beside the barbecue holding a pair of tongs. He has been tasked with cooking our meal. I notice that, although he is dutifully flipping the chicken, his gaze is fixed—contemplative.

God bestows us, His children, with the ability to dive deep into our own minds. This gift, like so many others, is often present from a very young age, when simple answers from our parents prove utterly dissatisfying. God crafts simple thinkers, placing in their hands oars that they may row peacefully along the waters, blissfully content, asking little about what lurks below. In the much the same way, He creates, and then submerges, complex thinkers to plumb great depths and decipher exactly what treasures lay buried on the ocean floor. Unlike humans, who show favouritism toward one disposition or the other, the good Father takes equal pleasure in His creations and has the same great plans for both types of thinkers.

I watch Sam rise from the depth of the thought he's just completed to the surface, and our eyes meet. A sudden sensation shoots through my arm and up my neck, causing both eyelids to flutter.

"Kerri!" My friend, Lisa, jabs me hard in the ribs and causes my cheek to dawn their rosy Irish hue. "It's been fun, but I've got an exam tomorrow. Are you okay to drive me home?"

"Yes, of course," I reply. Yet long after I've packed up my things and we are driving home, I still feel the warmth of Sam's eyes centred on me.

"You like him, don't you?" Lisa asks from the passenger seat, a crooked smile meandering its way across her lips.

"No," I say defensively. It's a lie that my anxious heart wants so badly to believe.

"Okay," she says and stares at me a moment longer before she looks away. Good friends read faces and body language, not words, because our gestures often hold the truth we are not ready to express.

"We're very different people," I continue, my words turning to thought as I desperately try to convince my mind what my heart won't budge on.

Sam and I grew up in vastly different worlds, which laid down the paths we trod upon our first glorious tastes of freedom.

Sam began his adult life sprinting on a gravel road away from his father's alcoholism, stones flying underfoot. The major assets to his name were resilience and the general idea that life is what you make of it, so he'd better make it good. This worldview, alongside his likeable personality, intelligence, and work ethic, made him a popular teammate. Sam's innate running talent afforded him the luxury of attending university. He was cognizant of this privilege and desired to use his schooling well by pursuing science and mathematics.

On the other hand, the road onto which my feet fell in an easy stride was paved with privilege and opportunity. Despite struggling with an eating disorder early on in my adolescence, my parents' love and support laid down a secure path for me. Running and academic scholarships, coupled with my parents diligent saving, ensured my schooling was mostly paid for.

Long after I dropped Lisa off at home, my mind remained unsettled. Were we really that different after all, I pondered. Or was the only significant difference between Sam and I exposure to the world? I had led a fairly sheltered childhood and teenage years, never having walked in a drunken stupor or even felt the rush of emotion when kissing a boy. Sam, on the other hand, had experienced much, and only now do I know that he experienced much more than he ever cared to. Isn't it true that, in our society, people rarely worry about starvation? The greater issue is that they have stuffed themselves to the brim with the things of the world and are sick from indigestion.

I did not know how to reconcile our differences, having thumbed through the gold-tipped pages of my Bible enough times to know that God warns us, "*Do not be unequally tied with unbelievers...*" (2 Corinthians

6:14). Is that what Sam was? An unbeliever? I had never asked him, so how could I be sure? Why had God allowed him to show up so centrally in my life at such a critical juncture? Heaven knows I was not seeking a relationship at that time. Only a few months prior, I had broken off a relationship with a boy that was everything on paper that I thought God wanted for me. In reality, I had little desire to make our relationship work. It was a decision that left my mind reeling.

Lying awake that night, I decided to quell whatever emotions were causing my heart rate to rise at the mention of Sam's name. I could not date him. After all, it was against God's will and my better judgment. Wasn't it?

Three short months later, on a humid summer's evening, I pounded three flights of stairs to the top floor suite I shared with my best friend, Sara, in her dad's 100-year-old house. Flopping hard onto the mattress we had deliberately placed in the hallway between our two rooms, I exhaled wildly. She heard me open the door and friendship intuition told her I had news she didn't want to miss. After our second summer living in this arrangement, it didn't take long for us to determine our busy schedules mandated that we organize a daily time to catch up on life. And so, almost every night, before we crawled into our own beds to escape the exhaustion of summer jobs, university classes, training schedules, and boys, we would spend anywhere from five minutes to five hours sharing our stories in the mattress fort we had erected between our two rooms.

"What is it?" she asked expectantly, with an enthusiasm impossible to ignore. How is it that best friends are dialed into your thoughts in a way that cannot be demystified? How many times has a text come in, or a phone call or an email, that related precisely to how you were feeling without even the slightest hint at the day's reckonings? I suppose the answer may be that God often chooses to use people to do His work. Life lived without intercession and wise counsel would be nothing short of catastrophic.

"He kissed me," I said between giddy gulps of air.

"He whaattt?" She shrieked with both delight and disbelief.

"I mean it was kind of a kiss. A half cheek kind of kiss. Oh, Sara... I must be the most awkward person on the planet at this." I shook my head in an effort to slough off the embarrassment I felt.

"You see, I panicked and might have completely dodged it, and..." I buried my head in the blanket beneath us and inhaled its familiar scent of trusted friendship.

"Oh, Kerri, it's okay." Her words were gentle and sincere and extended me the confident acceptance of not needing to hide.

I peered back up at my friend who had come to know me so well.

"What do I do?" The phrase escaped from somewhere inside of me and trailing behind, like smoke, all the confusion I had been feeling over a boy I was not supposed to love. My heart was yearning for a companion I barely knew.

"I think you date him," she responded, measured and even—everything I couldn't be in this exhilarating moment.

"My parents won't understand," I said as my mind rode the swell of fear to its likely conclusion—my parents would disapprove of this unchurched suitor

"Sam deserves a chance, Kerri. Your parents deserve a chance too," Sara stated. Her eyes gripped my own in a sincerity that could not easily be disregarded.

I rolled onto my back and stared at the intricate crown moulding above us. My Creator, the one who first formed Adam and saw that it was not good for him to be alone, seemed to have created me with a similar void.

It's Saturday afternoon, and I am thumbing through my Bible, pages known and worn in a similar fashion as the couch that cradles me. I'm writing this section and still grasping at straws when it comes to tracing the hand of God in each detail of my relationship with Sam.

Remarkably, today marks our eleventh-year wedding anniversary, the day we stood before God and uttered promises far more profound than our twentysomething-year-old selves were capable of fathoming. All we held, besides each other's hands, was a love God used to transform us both—the sharp angles of our hearts rounded by the sanding block of covenant. We fumbled around for some time in our oversized commitment, as if we were wearing shoes too big for of us to fill, before our gracious Father revealed to us the essence of relationship. And what greater means would He use, but the love we were both learning to stretch and accommodate for each other? As it turns out, remaining faithful to a promise, in good or bad, in sickness or in health, carries within it the power to change the whole world.

On June 9, 2007, our potential far outreached our position. Yet, as I think back to our beginnings, when our two souls chaffed against holiness, I can't help but wonder, *Did God account for our mistakes in His over-arching plan? Or is every human error a detour on an undetermined path that God allowed me to procure?*

The legalistic side of me ruminates once more on Paul's words to the Corinthians, when my fingers stumble across Hosea, and the Spirit stirring within me gives me pause. As I dive into the words that lay bare before me, bits of the unconventional story come flooding back to my memory.

The Lord instructs Hosea to take a wife that none would expect him to take, and, beyond all reason, Hosea loves her faithfully. In doing so, he serves as an example of the way the Lord loves His wayward children for the rest of humanity.

This story, and many more like it, can make God seem faltering in His commands. We are to be set apart, a holy priesthood, unyoked to unbelievers, and yet he commands His beloved prophet to marry a prostitute.

I am struck once more by the way our knowledge of God seldom needs to be narrowed down or boxed in with stand-alone verses, but rather expanded upon and erected, like a bridge, with pillar upon biblical pillar to support the entire expanse of His character. He desires that we know His character through the almost one million written words He gifted us and by the careful involvement and work of His Spirit in our lives. The sheer number of words declare that there is infinitely more to discover about God than most of us ever dare to experience.

Scripture clearly reveals a God capable of preordaining relationships *and* redeeming them. He seldom works within our "either / or" confines. Our job on earth is not to figure God out, but rather to follow Him and submit to Him as Leader and Lord.

Please do not misread what I am saying through my story or Hosea's. Dating is not a game, and I am not passing star-crossed lovers a free pass past *Go*, nor am I encouraging Christ followers to seek out relationships with non-believers. I believe there is sufficient evidence in the Bible to suggest that marrying someone who does not share your beliefs will cause heartache and unnecessary trouble.

That is not what happened between Sam and me. By the time we exchanged rings and vows, he had given his heart to Jesus, was baptized into the family of Christ, and was walking in step with the Holy Spirit.

What I am saying is that, whether my heart was supernaturally open to this relationship before these steps were taken, or if God, instead, needed to engage in the process of redeeming two broken people, makes little difference *now*. For God works in a multitude of ways, and trying to make sense of every intricate detail may never do His good work justice or give Him the glory He so richly deserves. Suffice it to say, we often do more harm by judging others before the Holy Spirit had has a chance to do His powerful redemptive work. Instead, each of us should seek to do what God has asked us to do in accordance with His will and the instruction manual He sent us. The key is reading the manual. All of it. And often.

St. Augustine knew this all too well. This man breathed scripture in so deeply that almost every sentence he breathed out was scented with its unmistakable fragrance. How my heart longs to live that way, viewing everything through the love extended to us in Jesus Christ. I long for God's word to be in my vision constantly, that, even when the book is removed, every word hangs in the air like spectacles, imperative to my very act of seeing.

I did follow Sara's advice from that warm summer night and acted upon the curiosity saturating my thoughts. I dated Sam. And his love began to mirror back to me the immeasurable love and all-encompassing acceptance available through Jesus Christ. I had not yet learned how to experience the fullness of this love—I was too busy stumbling on account of it. But praise be to God for sending Sam to me. His love proved to be a powerful antibiotic; it courageously fought the infectious lies that had been whispered to me by the adversary.

For isn't it true that in our time of greatest need, God sent a person? His son.

Chapter Ten

blinded by the veil

I strain to look forward,
eyes blinded to see,
even though reality
is right in front of me.

I'm groping for purpose.
I'm striving for praise.
Yet I'm missing the love
that cracked open the grave.

Will somebody see me,
and loosen the ties
wound around my face,
and veiling my eyes?

After successfully rehabilitating my legs from the blow of three stress fractures, the summer of 2005 boasted a great victory in my track and field career. I ran a flawless 10,000-metre race to win the silver medal at the Canada Games in Regina, Saskatchewan. Being near the top of my game gratified my desire to succeed. I was once again on track to achieve *my* purpose—my worth.

The term, "runner's high" has been circulating for some time, and it is due to the biological response to exercise, which unleashes the body's production of endorphins. An article by *CNN* quotes J. Kip Matthews, a sport and exercise psychologist, who explains it like this: "Endorphins, which are structurally similar to the drug morphine, are considered natural painkillers because they activate opioid receptors in the brain that help minimize discomfort."[16]

The wounds my soul carried cried out for relief, and running provided a powerful drug to numb the pain—if only for thirty-seven minutes. I stayed focused on controlling external circumstances to ease the discomfort within my soul, or pursued success to avoid it altogether, rather than deal with the root cause of it. I was unable to muster the courage to peer behind the gauze I had haphazardly applied. Even so, God was patient with me, waiting for me to grow in maturity before revealing what seriousness lurked behind the veil.

Peter, in defence of the mockers who asked why Jesus had not yet come, describes God's character as *forbearing*, which means "patient" or "restrained." God was waiting for me to discover the problem with veiling or coping—that my runner's high would eventually dissipate and I would remain unchanged, wailing over the same raw wounds.

We live across the bridge from the downtown area of our city. Every Saturday morning, like clockwork, men circle our neighbourhood, skin cracked by the blistering sun, with garbage bags and shopping carts hoping to collect the remains of the rich man's Friday night coping ritual. These men pound the streets each week, collecting bottles to sell and then buying their own coping mechanism of choice.

The irony of this twisted symbiotic relationship is that God created our world to thrive within cycles—for one organism to benefit merely by another's existence. When sin broke our world, it broke our cycles and twisted the very essence of benefit. To help another cope is not true benefit, and yet the courage it would take to break these twisted cycles is beyond what most of us could muster. What if the sound of Friday nights was the clink of two fragile hearts soberly confessing hard truths? Why, instead, do we cling to momentary pleasure and worship it in place of God, our highest good?

Dr. Paul Brand, the son of missionary parents turned doctor, proved that "leprosy does not cause the 'rotting away' of the hands and feet.

Instead it is the loss of sensation which makes people affected by leprosy prone to injuring themselves."[17] His research proved the need for sensation and pain as essential elements of our overall health. We need to feel where we are injured in order to properly address the wound and take steps toward healing. In Dr. Brand's later days, he wrote a book titled, *Pain: The Gift Nobody Wants*. Isn't this profoundly true? Pain is a gift that we treat like a nuisance, a burden that we foolishly believe will only hold us back, rather than propel us forward into profound healing and health.

Standing on the podium at the Canada Games with a silver medal draped proudly around my neck, I spotted my parents in the crowd with little effort. My dad's freckled fingers were wrapped tight around the video camera obstructing his face, yet nothing could hide his wide grin. My mom was snapping pictures relentlessly, always one to attempt to capture the moment just as it felt in her heart—perfect. The distance between our physical bodies was maybe forty feet, yet the chasm between our hearts felt farther than the fourteen laps I had just run. Having partitioned myself from them by my own hand-sewn veils, I continued to give ear to the adversary's lies, compelling me to keep steeping my identity in accomplishment. After all, my parents could never fully understand my distorted body-image and subsequent need to earn my self-worth. As a parent now myself, I know just how deceptive this lie was because there is nothing my children could ever do to keep me from loving them. No wound, however invasive, could repel this mother's love. If they find themselves in trouble, they need only say the word—and I will run, or drive, or fly, or climb a mountain in the dead of night to come to their aid.

The people I needed the most to help me step out onto the water and walk toward Christ were the very people I was pushing away. Yet, in God's providence, He had situated another person in my life who might encourage me to find my prize in Christ, someone who might encourage me to take my eyes off the waves and, instead, look to Him.

I needed to be shown that, in hiding behind my veils like a fearful child, I was foolishly separating myself from a loving Father who knew how to work *all* things for my good (Romans 8:28), the One who knew my heart (Psalm 44:21) and how greatly it had been deceiving me (Jeremiah 17:9). God had not abandoned me—it was shame that caused me to run. All throughout God's continued pursuit of me, I had become wholly unaware that the darkness I thought I saw was really just my own blindness.

Chapter Eleven

sedimentary rock

Pebble upon pebble,
sand upon sand,
pressure, compaction:
now there is land.

It seems to be sturdy,
it's holding my weight.
I don't heed the warning:
"Weak foundation. May break."

I TAUGHT ELEMENTARY SCHOOL FOR FOUR YEARS BEFORE MY HUSBAND AND I decided that I would stay home to care for our little family full-time. I particularly enjoyed teaching the science unit on rocks and minerals. I loved explaining the rock cycle to my students because it was almost always new information for them. As a Manitoba teacher who grew up in this province made up mostly of sedimentary rock, I took great care in teaching the fascinating way in which this type of rock is formed.

If I close my eyes and lift my hands, I can almost retrace the exact movements involved in drawing the infamous rock cycle diagram. First, the rocky cliffs exemplifying the Canadian Shield terrain with arrows swooping down the hills, representing the wind and rain eroding away the rock in the same fashion a that carpenter might sand down a good piece of wood. Next, the arrows that depict the sediment being swept away by powerful waters, the grain's own will bent by a greater power toward a greater purpose.

Isn't this precisely the way God often works in our lives? Master, even over our brokenness, guiding it toward an extraordinary purpose.

What comes next in the diagram, and in our lives, is often what seems the most catastrophic. However, this process is utterly imperative to the creation of something new. The thick, black down-pointing arrows signifying that the sediment must sink deep into the sea without the foresight to know what will become of it.

Even in the rock cycle—an undeniably scientific process—God's truth is embedded like a thumbprint. We too must first die to ourselves if we are to become something new in Christ (2 Corinthians 5:17), the sediment of our hopes and dreams sinking deep into the unknown, while we cling to the providential plans of our Masterful Creator. For when we reach the bottom of the ocean or the end of ourselves, as the sediment always does, it is then and only then that new rock can form. Here the words of Jesus' own disciples ring ever true: "*...this is a hard saying; who can listen to it?*" (John 6:60).

In October of the following training year, I was in peak physical condition. All signs pointed to a victorious cross country season, one in which I would more than likely stand on top of the podium as one of the best runners in the Canadian University circuit. Every Sunday, my eight-mile-long run felt effortless and supremely satisfying. My performance was finally beginning to align with all the talent my coaches proclaimed.

On the bus ride out to Edmonton for a routine five-kilometre meet, I felt a familiar pain creeping up the outside of my leg. I brushed it off and cranked *Dashboard Confessional* even louder in my headphones, their passionate melodies the soundtrack to my pursuit. I refused to let any type of negative thought cloud my pre-racing mind.

The next day, when I stepped onto the start line, I knew I wouldn't finish the race. I bowed out at three kilometres with a throbbing leg and a fractured heart. That was one of the last races I ever competed in on a national stage.

Upon returning from the meet, I was diagnosed with yet another stress fracture. Nine weeks after, I suffered from tendinitis in my Achilles tendon that was so severe I had to cut slits in the back of my running shoes just to make it from my car to my classes on campus without doubling over in excruciating pain. A week or two after the swelling in my tendons began to subside, I developed plantar fasciitis in both of my feet. For several months, I slept with braces that kept my feet fully extended at night in order for them to heal.

During this time, my sports physician prescribed me powerful anti-inflammatories for months on end that slowly burned a hole in my stomach, causing internal bleeding—something I hadn't bargained for while I sought relief from my swelling Achilles.

In a span of eight months, my dreams of winning gold at the Canadian Interuniversity Sport Championships lay like organic sediment on the bottom of a cold, dark, ocean floor. Over countless nights, I called out to God in agony over my situation only to feel the weight of the ocean above me and hear its insulating power against my own voice.

I prayed reverently for healing, believing with the Spirit who still resided in me that the Lord was able—yet healing never came. Like many others who find themselves groping on the ocean floor for the pieces of a dream they once carried, I began to falsely assume my voice was incapable of slicing through the miles of water above me. The heaviness of the water above, meant to be harnessed for His good transforming work, felt like it was slowly suffocating me.

Even though I was trying to look up from down below, I did not know that I was still veiled and blind to God's truth for me. Draped over my eyes and the wounds of my soul were layers of control, avoidance, and doubt that distorted my faith, leading me to believe that God was not good—at least not good to me. Why would He allow all of these physical obstacles if He cared about my dreams or desires? This God, who was supposed to be my Abba Father, felt incredibly distant, cruel, and unloving.

I confessed these thoughts to no one for they were too unfiltered, too raw. The thought of God became burdensome. I prayed out of duty, not love. Shortly thereafter, my thoughts began to stray, like the prodigal son, believing joy was out *there*, not within the inner recesses of my soul.

Heading down a winding road in the opposite direction than God had called me to go, I made compromises that I should not have. I sought fulfillment in lesser things—being a *good* girlfriend and a fun friend. Lines that, at one time, I would have deemed black and white all took on a greyish hue. I refused to let go of *my* dreams. Despite my fractured bones, I did my best to convince those around me that the Kerri everyone loved remained intact. It became my mission to make sure no one sensed the chaotic seas churning within my soul. Mine was a silent, largely undramatic, deeply personal rebellion. Even though my faith was sinking, I waved no flags and sounded no warning calls.

My saving grace came when God beached my proverbial ship. Due to my inability to compete, I no longer travelled with the track team on weekends. Therefore, I found myself back at church. That church—Oasis Community Church—originated out of a close-knit Italian community and housed about sixty to seventy people each Sunday morning for its English service led by a young, passionate pastor. My brother and I drove there in our gas guzzler that nearly broke the bank with every fill, but it got us there—it got *me* there. That fact alone is yet another example of the power of intercession, proof that God's ears are attuned to the groaning Spirit inside every mother and father, who only want the best for their children. And, just as Jesus once turned water into wine, God is more than able to miraculously turn our helplessness into His sovereign action. We need not give in to despair.

One ordinary autumn day fairly early on in my relationship with Sam, while hanging out around the track, he asked me a question that changed the course of both of our lives.

"What are you doing on Sunday?" he asked rather casually, while stretching his calves on the calf board. He had just finished a workout, one I had watched with equal parts fascination and jealousy. He had the same competitive fire pulsating through his veins. He loved to push the limits of his body's capacity with almost as much zeal as me. Witnessing that in someone I was starting to love was almost as good as experiencing it for myself. *Almost*.

"I don't know," I replied. "Going to church in the morning with my brother like usual, I guess."

I stared down at my feet, unable to bring myself to read his facial expressions when I said this. I felt too ashamed of the anarchy taking place my soul.

"You go to church every week..." he said carefully, prodding around my veils, searching for the light he'd seen shine through.

He continued, "And you've never invited me to go. When are you going to invite me to go?" His tone was serious, yet his flirtatious grin assured me I didn't need to be afraid of his heartfelt curiosity.

Before I had the chance to audibly respond to Sam's question, I felt what can only be described as the Spirit inside me leaping for joy. Elizabeth recounts this very phenomenon when she greets Mary, pregnant with the saviour of the world.

My soul, still anchored to truth through the Holy Spirit's presence, knew how significant his curiosity was. Despite a sudden surge of emotion almost rendering me mute, the Holy Spirit calmly and confidently provided the words eluding me.

I drew in this Spirit-inspired confidence before breathing out the words in a voice only decibels above a quiet whisper: "Do you want to go with me?" I turned away slightly as I asked, attempting to evade the man who was gently tugging at my threads, unknowingly threatening to unravel the tapestry of lies that was shrouding my soul. I was suddenly more afraid of the answer than the question itself.

Up until this point, my reasons for not inviting Sam to church had become two-dimensional. On one hand, I did not want to be in a relationship with someone who believed in God simply because his girlfriend did. The desire to be with someone who desperately wanted Jesus for Himself, not for the spouse it might offer him, was deeply ingrained in me. On the other hand, my faith had been faltering over the past few months, and I had taken some pleasure in the autonomy doubt provides.

Before I had a chance to brace myself for the implications of his response, Sam confidently replied, "Yes, I think I do."

I have no doubt that, the very moment Sam uttered those words, a chorus of angels, led by God Himself, filled the heavens with strains of glorious delight. Far too often I have forgotten that God's prerogative is seeking and saving the lost. Jesus himself said, "*I have not come to call the righteous but sinners to repentance*" (Luke 5:32).

God knew the whole story He was in the midst of writing—even if I didn't have a clue. And He was eagerly waiting for me, with colourful robe and fattened calf in hand, for all that was to come.

In Acts 9, we read about Saul's acceptance of Christ and the restoration of his physical sight. Saul was an early persecutor of the Christian Church, and, according to him, one of the worst (1 Timothy 1:15). Acts 9 describes the details of Saul's encounter with the risen Christ on a road near Damascus, after which he is rendered blind.

After the encounter with Saul, God gives a message to a man named Ananias to lay his hands on Saul and restore his sight. Ananias is astounded at the Lord's request, refuting back, "*...Lord, I have heard from many about this man, how much evil he has done to your saints at Jerusalem*" (Act 9:13).

God insists, telling Ananias, *"...Go, for he is a chosen instrument of mine to carry my name before the Gentiles and kings and the children of Israel. For I will show him how much he must suffer for the sake of my name"* (Acts 9:15–16).

The story continues:

> *So Ananias departed and entered the house. And laying his hands on him he said, "Brother Saul, the Lord Jesus who appeared to you on the road by which you came has sent me so that you may regain your sight and be filled with the Holy Spirit." And immediately something like scales fell from his eyes, and he regained his sight...*
>
> —Acts 9:17–18

I always thought scales were gross. I thought they were slimy and repulsive to the touch. On the contrary, I now understand the beautiful metaphor pictured here. First of all, fish scales are, according to scientists, "permanent on fish skin."[18] They are not meant to come off; the removal of scales is a miracle in and of itself. Secondly, "the bright metallic sheen of fish skin—source of endless fascination for fishermen and aquarium owners—is due to a sophisticated system of crystals that enhance light reflection."[19] When viewed in this regard, scales falling from someone's eyes and catching the light on their way down is truly a miraculous moment of beauty. Every conversion is.

A few short weeks after our conversation at the track, I witnessed Sam's conversion. And, for a time after that, Sam and I existed inside an upside-down relationship, carried gracefully by the Author of our story. While I felt buried under miles of ocean water, pressed down on every side, Sam, having surrendered his life to Christ, experienced a great weight being lifted from him. I watched as God accomplished in Sam's life what He has done since the dawn of creation—form together pieces of dust into a new being.

One evening, a few months later, I was over at Sam's apartment. We had just finished eating homemade pizza when Sam ushered me to the couch, where we sat down across from one another. The sombre expression on his face told me our conversation was about to take a turn. I could no longer ignore the darkening clouds on our horizon.

"You have something you need to tell me," I said, the first one to point my finger at the storm.

He shifted his weight and looked down.

I touched his chin with my finger and ever so gently lifted his head.

"It's okay," I assured him. "I can handle it."

This was a half truth at best. I had feared this moment ever since I felt myself fall in love with him. I knew there were secrets lurking in his past that might undo me, and I did not think I could face the consequences associated with knowing the truth. Even so, percolating beneath the words I had spoken was a supernatural courage that steadied my resolve.

He drew in a deep breath and, upon exhale, the stories began to spill out, confession upon confession, sin upon sin, until I stood beneath the waterfall of his words—completed drenched.

I remember what happened next as if it were yesterday. I slipped the diamond engagement ring he had given me just a few months previously off my finger and put it on the couch beside me, tears welling up in my eyes.

"I don't think I can do this. I don't think we are going to make it," I said, not believing it but desperately wanting to escape the pain of *knowing* his every secret and every wound. And then came the moment that changed everything. The moment that changed me.

With unwavering confidence, Sam looked me in the eyes and said, "Okay, I don't expect you to bear all of this." The pause that followed seemed to stretch, and then Sam cut straight through the silence with words more courageous and battle-worthy than I've ever uttered myself.

He said, "I want you to know, even if you walk away from this relationship right now, I will not stop following Jesus. I am a different person because of who you introduced me to, and I thank you for that."

In that hallowed moment, the Holy Spirit lifted the veils covering my soul to hear and understand a profound realization: Jesus came for the broken. He came for those who *realize* their need for Him. Sam had found Jesus by embracing his brokenness, not despite it.

Rather than owning my own brokenness, I was hell-bent on veiling it. But God, in His great wisdom, gifted me with a front row seat to a true conversion so that I may experience a conversion of my own. My Father saw through my Pharisaical facade that was fixated on the speck in Sam's eye and loved me enough to show me the log lodged in my own.

Sedimentary rock is built by small deposits of sediment over time. Sedimentary faith is built by small deposits of half-truths. No matter the formation process, the end result is the same: rock is formed, or faith is built. It is in the testing of the rock, however, when we discover exactly what it is made of.

Chapter Twelve

igneous rock

The finer the grind,
the purer the stone,
recasting my image
to mirror His own.

As a child, I spent at least two weeks every summer exploring the islands and natural beaches of Dogtooth Lake, nestled within the majestic Canadian Shield. Most of my camping days involved arising far too early to devour a book in the company of songbirds. After that, I would venture out on the water in the bow of my parents' fishing boat, the breeze stroking my face like gentle hands, while I watched the sun dance upon pristine waters.

My time spent on that boat formed me in the same way a file glides across soapstone, etching out its creation. Each summer I visited this sacred place, all the hardships were filed away and smoothed out. At Dogtooth Lake, I became my simplest and best form.

Here on this lake, I was perfectly cradled in the safety of the cliffs that surrounded me, a mirror image of my heavenly Father that He wanted to brand upon my heart. The magnetic pull I felt to the Canadian Shield was really my heaven-spun desire to build my life upon the one true rock.

All along, I knew I needed God. I knew, based on the truths taught to me as child, that if my life were to stand up to natural disasters, I needed to build it upon a solid rock. What I had not figured out until this point in my life was that I was building my foundation on the wrong type of rock. The rock I had chosen was, at its core, glorified sand.

After Sam and I were married, I continued to wrestle with physical injury. I felt as if my body had been plagued—cursed. Although I greatly desired to return to competitive sport, the tendinitis in my Achilles persisted like a bad cough, and the plantar fasciitis shot pain through my heel with every step. Weeks turned into months, and months soon became a year. Despite physiotherapy, message therapy, and no running, I was unable to return to training. During this season, deferred hope proliferated like weeds amidst the garden of my soul—crowding out joy with anger. I was angry over my shattered dreams, angry at the people I loved for not being able to help me, angry at myself for not being able to accomplish what I had set out to do, and most of all, angry at God for what I perceived was Him letting me down.

I heard a psychologist once say something along the lines of this: the angriest people in the world are, at their core, wild optimists. Anger is simply their response to the ecstatic hopes that have died an excruciating death. This anger, or veil of doubt, kept me from seeing that the celestial wrestling match in which my body was participating was an attempt to slough off and file down the soapstone of my soul to its best form.

Brother Lawrence, a monk well-known for being a practitioner of God's presence, was born to peasant parents in 1611.[20] While serving in army as a young man, he experienced a powerful vision, which granted him "supernatural clarity into a common sight."[21] This vision is described in a collection of his conversations and letters, gathered by a colleague, entitled *The Practice of the Presence of God*:

> That in the winter, seeing a tree stripped of its leaves, and considering that within a little time the leaves would be renewed, and after that the flowers and fruit appear, he received a high view of the providence and power of God, which has never since been effaced from his soul. That this view had perfectly set him loose from the world, and kindled in him such a love

> for God that he could not tell whether it had increased during the more than forty years he had lived since.[22]

Brother Lawrence went on to live and serve in a monastery as a kitchen worker for some time. When his physical disability, sustained from his time in war, became too cumbersome for kitchen labour, he spent years joyfully fixing sandals. This man, who spent much of his life dedicated to the act of being steeped in the divine presence, says this about the purpose behind *some* physical maladies: "He often sends diseases of the body to cure those of the soul."[23]

Having not been transformed by a vision like Brother Lawrence, I remained unable to peel back the veils to see, with God's eyes, the soul injuries He desired to heal and redeem for His purposes. Instead, deterred only by the physical injury itself, I shifted my focus towards pursuing a career in teaching.

Having tasted much success and fulfillment from my earlier babysitting days, and then again in each summer job I worked instructing children, I sensed teaching would be a good fit for me. Everyone in my life wholeheartedly supported my decision to pursue this new direction. After graduation, I quickly landed a temporary position at a public elementary school. Each morning, I showed up to my classroom just after 7:00 a.m., planned and prepped, and then the show began at 8:30 a.m., when the students arrived. I dramatized and emphasized and did just about anything, except stand on my head, to help them learn. When the production ended at 3:30 p.m., I poured over every detail and modified the next day's lessons until 4:30 or 5:00 p.m. Once home, I would grade assignments and compose parent emails until late in the night, and then wake up to do it all over again.

Although the students liked me and I received positive feedback on multiple occasions from my principal, I still doubted my abilities and my students' progress. There was simply no way of knowing if I measured up, if I was doing *enough*.

Near the end of the year, the principal of the prestigious private school where I had student-taught called me and said she had a permanent Grade Four teaching position for which she wanted me to interview. I was elated. Permanent positions were hard to attain. I knew many teachers who spent five or six years bouncing around from term to term, teaching different grades or at different schools each year. I did not think I could handle this kind of turbulence in the public school system, so I jumped at the opportunity.

Pulling up to the campus, with its stoic buildings framed by a canopy of ancient oak trees and overlooking one of Winnipeg's iconic rivers, I was quickly reminded of the prestige this place encapsulated. I knew that having a job at this school would elicit respect, which only made me desire the position more.

One week later, I received a call from the principal offering me the job. Fear quickly displaced elation, and I wondered how I would ever live up to their mantra of "striving for excellence." I did not see myself as innately excellent; how could I go about cultivating that confidence among twenty, nine-year-olds?

Despite my growing anxiety over my new job, I pressed on. I believed my goal of achieving worth was entirely possible, especially when working for such a prestigious private school. I spent the entire summer prepping in order to attain my new goal. I organized and reorganized, planned and replanned, and agonized over every single detail of my never-perfect-enough classroom. I even set up an aquarium, which boasted an assortment of tropical fish, in order to set a fun and inspiring mood for my classroom.

Ironically, I did all this before the painters checked off the box that said Room 218. One morning, I opened up my classroom door to find every poster I had painstakingly hung scattered like shells on the seashore. Tragically, all six of my gorgeous tropical fish were belly up, having ingested a toxic bouquet of paint fumes throughout the night. I didn't know whether to laugh or cry. I am pretty sure I did both. Little did I know that God has a sense of humour about how much I think I can control. He must scratch his head at our failure to understand just how much we have to learn.

Well over 2000 years ago, a woman named Martha struggled with this same tendency—believing she knew enough already. She had been rushing about her home all morning, scrubbing pots, prepping food, checking and re-checking her checklist—she *knew* what it took to entertain guests. And all morning her sister, Mary, had been sitting at the feet of Jesus, *doing nothing*. After passing by her sister for the twentieth time, her nerves were sufficiently grated and she could no longer stay silent. So she said, "*...Lord, do you not care that my sister has left me to serve alone?*" (Luke 10:40). Her misconception in regards to what Mary was *doing* was cleared up when Jesus replied: "*...Martha, Martha, you are anxious and troubled about many things, but one thing is necessary. Mary has chosen the good portion, which will not be taken away from her*" (Luke 10:41–42).

Mary had positioned herself as learner, not "one who already knew." Her ears were open to what Christ might teach her. She was not set in her ways. Martha, on the other hand, foolishly believed she already knew what needed to be done. She was focused on her perspective—not Christ's.

I muscled my way through that first year of teaching and collapsed on my backyard lawn chair when summer finally offered me an escape. That's the thing about striving: no matter what you achieve, it will never set you free. Rather, it seeks to own you by establishing your identity in what you've accomplished—which is never enough. I think I took four weeks out of ten off before I was back to the grind again. I spent day after day sitting in my classroom, reinventing the educational wheel, which, in actuality, was really just a personal attempt to reinvent me.

My principal happened to be at the school one summer day and called me into her office. I sat down, optimistic about a conversation regarding my obvious work ethic. How quickly the tables turned on me.

Her usually peppy voice turned serious as soon as I entered the room. "Kerri, I am going to give you a letter from a parent of one of your students from last year," she said. "I want you to read it, and after you read it, I want you to throw it in the garbage." Her face took on a look of pity, a look that said, *I can see you are trying so hard, you poor thing*. I wasn't just trying hard, I was trying my *hardest*.

Taking the letter in my heads, I recognized the last name, and my heart sank. I had deeply cared for the boy and his family. I had given them my all. Reading the subject line, I quickly surmised what this was all about. This student, to his parents' dismay, did not appear to be academically gifted. To ease the pain of this disappointment, they drove perfectionist behaviour into him like it was his only lifeline. The general learning behaviour comments I wrote on the front of his report card each term were like a championship wrestling belt—hard fought for and greatly exalted.

Having taught this boy for the whole year, I will admit, at first glance, he did seem perfect. But, I slowly began to notice something that clicked all the puzzle pieces of his academic difficulties into place. When I was teaching, he listened, but not *really* listened. His body language said he was listening—legs crossed and face upturned toward me—yet over time I noticed that his eyes wore a waxed glaze. In actuality, when I was teaching, he was absorbing very little. By the time I realized this, he was two perfect terms in, and I faced a difficult decision. Did I give him the much anticipated and expected perfect behaviour report? Or did I provide honest feedback to parents who were already limping along with a fractured dream?

The page my principal handed me was long. The bold font further exaggerated the message the words were meant to carry. I'm sure to his parents my own report of their son had felt like an announcement of their apparent failure, rather than a window into his imperfectly perfect humanity. I wanted nothing more than to give them the opportunity to know and love their son in his true form. I wanted them to see his imperfections shine in the light of their graceful acceptance.

It seems paradoxical to me now that I was as reluctant as they were to receive the same the gift. God, the only One capable of comprehensively assessing my soul, longed to share with me His truthful report. And insomuch as I was trying to help these parents understand their child, God was extending to me a truthful assessment—my loves were disordered. My heart was captivated by other things *before* Him.

Gripping the letter between two clammy hands, I felt like a child standing on the edge of a ten-metre diving board. The Spirit, active and alive in me, was encouraging me to take the plunge, yet my flesh squirmed at the distance I would be required to fall. My principal motioned for me to open the letter, providing me the persuasion I needed to jump in, feet first.

To this day, I cannot recount one of the written words contained in that letter, meant to convince my principal of my total incompetence. However, I can tell you the words I saw etched upon the underside of my veils that day: *Worthless. Unqualified. Failure.*

It didn't matter that, by God's grace, I had mustered the courage to be a truth teller in a world of truth slayers—at least it didn't matter to these parents. And truth be told, in this moment, it didn't matter to me either. Their rejection felt like an unexpected blow, straight to my gut. It knocked my identity as an heir of Christ right out of me.

When our son turned five, we gave him a camera for his birthday. We were on a camping trip, and there was so much to capture. Squirrels, fires, and flowers filled his memory card faster than either of us thought possible. After much persuasion on his part, I pulled out our laptop, stashed away amidst our gear, and watched his pictures appear tiny file after tiny file before my eyes. I was struck by their authenticity. He had somehow managed to capture moments in time uncloaked in superficiality or appearances. His obvious height disadvantage allowed him to capture us and his world with a sense of grandeur. It made me think that the way I see myself and others is helplessly skewed.

If I could go back in time, I would tell my brand-new teacher self that failure was a part of the process and it did not define me—rather it would refine me. Then, perhaps, I would have seen myself in a different light. If only my twenty-four-year-old self could have glanced at my Father's film, perhaps the grandeur with which He captured me would have quelled the incessant urge to measure up.

According to Jesus, building my identity on my achievements was about as wise as building a house on sand. Ironically, when Jesus delivered this instructive message during one of His most famous teachings, the Sermon on the Mount, the very rock He was standing on, at the northern edge of the sea of Galilee, was basalt stone: "a dark-coloured, fine-grained, igneous rock..."[24]

If you remember anything at all from Grade Four science, you may recall that igneous rock is the strongest of the three main types of rock. Interestingly enough, the igneous rock on which Jesus stood was formed from by tiny eroded particles that were pressed down deep into the earth's fiery core.

I am going to hazard a guess that, from His vantage point on top of that hillside, Jesus knew exactly who He was speaking to. A talented orator speaks directly to his or her audience. Jesus was addressing the broken, the busted, the lowest of the low—the people whose lives had been ground down to almost nothing. Yet God with us, Emmanuel, standing on this solid igneous rock, bore witness to the fact that particles are refined in ways that only God the ironworker can orchestrate when they "go through the fire" as Isaiah prophesied. This highly pressurized process can cause these particles to form a magnificently strong rock—one that Jesus says we can build our lives on.

Christ came to show us that the way to Him begins with a life humbly broken down. The bits and pieces of who we once were must be reconstructed into who God, resurrected inside each of us, enables us to be. As Paul instructs, "*I have been crucified with Christ. It is no longer I who live, but Christ who lives in me…*" (Galatians 2:20).

Even though it felt like I was losing bits and pieces of my identity to the rushing waters ricocheting off my shore line, God was using this powerful process to erode away my faulty sedimentary foundation. The Creator, however, never stops at destruction. He allows it because He has already devised ways to weave it into His plan of redemption.

God was taking my eroded sediment that He may press it deep down into Himself and form in me a firm foundation—one as resilient and emboldened as igneous rock.

Chapter Thirteen

the crucifixion

As the nails drive in,
the Lamb supplies
a pardon for sinners
by innocence crucified.

The weight of my sin
holds Him there,
but I shed no tears
for the burden He bears.

I want the world;
I want Him not.
My ignorance costs Him
death on a cross.

How long will it take me
to see what I've done?
How long will I squander
the inheritance won?

Oh, how it moves me,
when my sight is restored:
the love of a saviour,
my undeserved reward.

My marriage is God's greatest earthly gift to me. When Sam and I wed, I was a mere shadow of the person I am today. The way God has woven together our stories serves as an ever-present reminder of His beautiful and mysterious works. The light that first shone through me and, in turn, lit up with love the dark crevices of Sam's heart, was the very same light I needed to be reflected back years later. I did not know that, in introducing Sam to God, he would reintroduce to me the very same God I had loved, yet scarcely knew.

During those first few impressionable years of marriage, when my physical injuries were as tender as the ones that marred my soul, Sam, filled with the love of Christ, devoted himself to my care. Each night, after we had plucked away on our university assignments and fuelled our bodies with whatever it was we could afford, Sam would sit next to me on our brown suede couch and offer to rub my feet, aching from plantar fasciitis. Every night, no matter how his day had gone, Sam would cradle my feet in his strong hands and break up the fibrous scar tissue that had accumulated. It was a simple gesture done with great love, through which God chose to bless me and use as a conduit for my physical healing.

Jesus knew the importance of simple gestures done with great love and intention. With his own crucifixion on the horizon of his view, Jesus chose with the little time he had left to wash His disciples' feet:

> *Now before the Feast of the Passover when Jesus knew that his hour had come to depart out of this world to the Father, having loved his own who were in the world, he loved them to the end. During supper when the devil had already put it into the heart of Judas Iscariot, Simon's son, to betray him, Jesus knowing that the Father had given all things into his hands, and that he had come from God and was going back to God, rose from supper. He laid aside his outer garments, and taking a towel, tied it around his waist. Then he poured water into a basin and began to wash the disciples feet and to wipe them with the towel that was wrapped around him. He came to Simon Peter, who said to him, "Lord, do you wash my feet?" Jesus answered him, "What I am doing you do not understand now, but afterward you will understand."*
>
> —John 13:1–7

Sam was modelling submission to my needs; I needed to learn submission to Christ. Yet, like Simon Peter, I was incapable of gleaning the truth that had grown into maturity before my very eyes. Still, in God's extravagant grace, he healed some of the ailments attacking my physical body, while allowing the seed of His truth to bury itself deep within the inner recesses of soul.

While the physical injuries subsided, living yoked to another also helped to keep me accountable to healthy eating. I learned, thanks to Sam's healthy perspective, what was rational and what was not. We planned meals together, shopped for groceries together, cooked together, and ate meals—now a time of holy communion—together. All this togetherness, in collaboration with sincere love, vanquished the lies I once believed about my body not measuring up. With Sam by my side, the dark behind the veils did not seem so threatening. The Psalmist words come to mind: "*Even the darkness is not dark to you; for the night is breath as the day, for darkness is as light with you*" (Psalm 139:12). God was not afraid of what I needed to face in my own soul. What I viewed as dark and in need of veiling, God saw as light, lying in wait for its appointed time to shine. Facing what lay dormant beneath the veils was the only way for me to be set free. And nine years later, this opportunity came.

Spring 2017 will be forever etched upon the tablet of my memory. The leaves popped early that year, proclaiming their new life, but my own life felt quite the opposite. I felt dry and brittle like fallen leaves on a cold autumn day. Although, I had developed the resolve needed to traverse mountains due to the numerous physical challenges I had faced in the past, the thought of the climb ahead overwhelmed me.

I lay on my back after yet another difficult morning navigating debilitating back and neck pain. It was Saturday and, thankfully, my husband was home with the kids. Instead of holding it together to make a decent lunch while the kids jostled and bickered, I was free to quietly retreat to my bedroom.

I had been to my doctor, multiple physiotherapists, massage therapists, and a chiropractor, each person entertaining different ideas of what was wrong with me—ideas that never seemed to ease the pain or explain my loss of function.

This new predicament was unwelcome, as I believed that my battle with physical injury was over. This pain was different from my previous running injuries. I could sense my mental and emotional composure unravelling. For five long months, despite my children sleeping through most nights, I struggled to stay asleep. I would wake up every hour, worrying incessantly about having enough strength to get through the day while successfully veiling my struggle from others. I came to dread the sound of my children's voice in the morning, bidding me to rise out of bed. The sweetness dripping from their raspy morning voices turned bitter in the midst of my newfound despair.

I have always *loved* children. I fed, burped, changed, and sang sweet lullabies to my toy babies faithfully in my childhood, with great anticipation of all that was to come. As soon as I became of age, I volunteered in my church nursery many Sundays. I played with any and all of the younger children in my neighbourhood. At family gatherings, I would willingly, and with great joy, babysit the younger cousins instead of goofing around with the cousins my age.

As an adult, little changed. Raising children with my husband was our greatest adventure together. I absolutely adored my two children, who were quickly approaching ages four and two. We had dreams of raising a large family, yet this unrelenting fog of pain and uncertainty about what was causing it was quickly causing these dreams to dissipate. The date my husband and I assigned to try for number three sailed by, leaving us questioning our once-certain future of three kids (or more)!

Looking up at the cracks in my bedroom ceiling that fateful spring day, with tears streaming down my face, I mouthed an anguished cry to the shadows, "God, why are you punishing me?"

Thanks to my front row seat and personal involvement in Sam's quest for God early on in our marriage, as well as other providential relationships through our church, I was growing closer to God rather than drifting away. I fully believed in His power to heal me, and I was not shy about pleading my cause before Him. In the same way that the persistent widow in one of Jesus' parables continually brought her case before the unjust judge, crying out "*...Give me justice against my adversary*" (Luke 18:3), I petitioned God daily for healing. Yet, no healing came. I could not help but feel the sting of rejection at what I assumed was God's unanswered promise, "*And will not God give justice to his elect, who cry to him day and night?*" (Luke 18:7). My faith, sprouting up in still-shallow soil, was quickly scorched by my own disappointment in an unjust God. This view of God became a jail cell, my sight impossibly obscured by its bars.

During this time, I found it difficult to enjoy being a mom with its exhaustive physical demands. There was always another bum to wipe, or problem to solve, or lunch to make—never mind the disastrous state of my house.

Further compounding my depressive state, I had recently given up my permanent teaching contract. In a single sentence—"I've decided to stay home with my children"—the career I had worked hard to obtain was over. If I wanted to go back to work (which currently seemed impossible), I would be starting over in the same way a new teaching grad might have to, subbing or taking terms as they presented themselves.

On that crescendo of a day, I stared at my ceiling a long time before I allowed the lurking shadows to crowd out the light. What was the point of this life I had anyway? Of living in pain. And being ignored by a God who, in my opinion, had proven Himself untrustworthy.

A dear person in my life told me my physical healing hinged entirely on my faith, which must be lacking. Her words left me deeply troubled, for, if there was one notion I possessed, it was that God could heal me. I had, many times, reached my hands into the air in fervent prayer, believing my fingers were within reach of the tip of His robe. No, I didn't doubt God's power to do good. Rather, I doubted God's power to do good in me. I was the problem. God had forsaken me.

I followed this rabbit hole of a thought until I reached its inevitable depths: If God had abandoned me, I should abandon myself as well. This thought brought with it an odd sense of comfort—the same sensation that swept me up in my eating disorder in the first place.

I know it now as deception, but at the time it disguised itself as desperation. Veiled from God's truth, I nursed the idea that I could be in control of my circumstances once more. After all, what good was a broken mommy to two very active and rambunctious kids? Wouldn't they just grow to resent their mommy, who was in undiagnosable pain? Would they succumb to the lie that my lack of faith put me in this position? What then of their faith?

I lay in my bed, held hostage by my own fear of the future. My time behind the veils had blinded me to the truth that Christ had already provided a way out. I couldn't see that, in my impatience, I had fashioned a golden calf, bowing to the feet of health, success, and status, instead of patiently waiting on the One True God.

And then, at precisely the right time, with a grace so undeserved, my Lord responded to my cries by pulling me from the miry bog of my despair and saving me in my powerlessness (Psalm 40:2 and Romans 5:6).

I heard the soft pad of footsteps up the stairs and, instinctively knowing it was a child, I pulled the covers over my swollen, tear-streaked face.

The door opened slowly and in walked my worker man, dressed in blazing yellow from head to toe. His glowing frame edged its way to the side of my bed, and he pressed his face so close that his warm breath dried my dewy cheeks.

"Mama?" he whispered gently, yet full of confidence.

He peeled the blankets away from my face, and, even though it pained me for him to see me in this state, I was powerless to stop him.

To my surprise, he did not balk when he saw me. In fact, it was as if nothing was wrong. I was the same mama to him then as I was when I joyfully lifted him up in an affectionate embrace.

"I made this for you," he whispered with a giddiness he could not hide. His hands opened up to reveal a Lego creation, which he carefully tucked beside my face.

"I love you, Mama."

His words filled the room long after he had slipped out. Curiosity gripped my thoughts and implored me to hold up his creation for examination. I did not recognize the gift I was holding and how God had used my own son as means to fulfill His sovereign plans.

My husband entered the room next, sitting on the edge of my bed close enough for him to stroke my face. As part of God's merciful plan, He provided an interpreter to explain the message He had sent me that I may rejoice in its good news. Thank God for the body of Christ. Thank God for courageous truth tellers and grace givers.

"Kerri, do you see, what our little worker man has made you?" he asked. "Do you see it?"

"Yes, I think it's an airplane or something," I mumbled, averting my eyes.

"No. No look again," he pressed, loving me enough to not let me fall off the edge head-first into temptation. It was my husband in that room, but God was also within him. I will never again forget that we are all extensions of Him. When people feel far from God, God in us can draw them close.

I looked long and hard at the blue, red, and yellow pieces crossing over each other in near perfect symmetry. Suddenly, a breath of Holy air swept across the room, lifting the veils. All at once, I saw what I had been blind to before. With emotion flooding my throat, I barely choked out the words to describe the miracle I now held—"It's... it's a cross."

Often, God draws most near when we feel the most forsaken by Him.

After Jacob deceitfully stole his brother's blessing, he was forced to flee Paddan-aram to find a wife. On his journey, one night while he slept, God sent him a power dream:

> *And he dreamed, and behold, there was a ladder set up on earth, and the top of it reached to heaven. And behold, the angels of God were ascending and descending on it! And behold, the Lord stood above it and said, "I am the Lord, the God of Abraham your father and the God of Isaac. The land on which you lie I will give to you and to your offspring. Your offspring shall be like the dust of the earth, and you shall spread abroad to the west and to the east and to the north and to the south, and in you and your offspring shall all the families of the earth be blessed. Behold,*

> *I am with you and will keep you wherever you go, and will bring you back to this land. For I will not leave you until I have done what I promised you."*
>
> —Genesis 28:12–15

Just as God kept his promise to Abraham through Isaac and Jacob, He fulfilled His promise to me. God sent Jacob the dream to dismantle his false belief that he could ascend his way to success—to God.

It was *through* the arresting absence I felt that God graciously communicated to me a message much like Jacob's. I now revel in the holiness of that moment with my son, drawing a divine parallel to Jacob's words from thousands of years before me, words spoken from the lips of a man who once cried out to the same immutable God: "*...Surely the Lord is in this place, and I did not know it*" (Genesis 28:16).

Chapter Fourteen

and the veil was to

A glorious thunder,
the veil split in two,
my soul bare before Him:
what's He to do?

Will He prod where I'm broken?
Will He poke where it's sore?
Will He laugh at my failures?
Will He call me a whore?

Yet, He binds up my wounds.
Yet, He breaks not my reed.
Yet, my wick He leaves burning,
acknowledging my need.

The God of all holies
is bending His knee.
The One who holds heaven
is instead holding me.

Jesus is the only human to have inhabited the earth fully embodying truth and, at the same time, fully dispensing grace. As believers in Christ, we are to follow His perfect example, yet most of us find ourselves incapable of consistently balancing the scales of truth and grace in our interactions with others.

I tend to lean heavily on the truth. Stubborn by nature, thanks to my Irish roots, I am able to confidently defend my case in front of others.

ents jest that I should have been a lawyer; I say that it is one of y jobs tucked safely in the front pockets of my "mom" apron, along-de nurse, teacher, chef, and counsellor.

I have hurt people I love dearly with my tendency towards poking and prodding. Rather than accepting another's flaws, or forgiving without requiring an explanation, as my husband seems to effortlessly do, I often want to expose the root of the sin—an excavation that is always painful and sometimes unnecessary. To this day, my husband still has to encourage me to tip my teetering words in the direction of grace.

Perhaps the reason I lean towards uncovering truth is because I lived beneath my own hand-spun veils for a very long time. Now I see that hiding my wounded soul prevented me from further intimacy with God. For far too long, I clung to a fraudulent existence because I was afraid to hold up the mirror and stare back at the girl who struggled with body image and fear—a girl who made idols out of achievement and success. Not only did I not want to face up to that girl, I cringed at the thought of *others* seeing her. My veils of control, avoidance, and doubt were merely a surgical drape used to protect me from God's scalpel of truth.

A.W. Tozer, a man whose writings have simultaneously challenged and encouraged me over the years, eloquently describes the veils I had willingly sewn in this way:

> It is not too mysterious, this opaque evil, nor it is hard to identify. We have but to look in our own hearts and we shall see it there, sewn and patched and repaired it may be, but there nevertheless, an enemy to our lives and an effective block to our spiritual progress.[25]

Very few of us would be eager to admit there is opaque evil lurking in or around our lives. After all, we should abhor evil—we should desire it uprooted from our society, our community, and our homes. Nonetheless, if we take an honest look at the person in the mirror, there we see it—the veil draped around our sinful condition perpetuating the lie that "there's nothing evil under *here*, all the evil that exists is out *there*."

Like Adam, we deflect ownership for evil in this world: "*...the woman whom you gave to be with me, she gave me the fruit...*" (Genesis 3:12), he cried, and our collective chorus echos the same. A most sinister kind of evil lurks in our blindness to our own condition, evil that pretends and defends its position as anything but. Like the adversary slithering around the garden as a snake, evil masks itself as non-existent, harmless, or even good, when in actuality it sweeps us down a river charged with the undercurrent of self exaltation that ultimately leads us to self destruction.

And yet, God is merciful, for He cannot be anything other than what He has always been. He looked down upon our sinful condition, our perpetual blindness, and simply could not forsake the beings He created. His love was greater than our doubt, His compassion more powerful than our selfishness. He saw with unclouded vision the way sin was destroying the world and knew He had to root it out. But to root out sin would require Him to root out the makers of sin, the people who first saw choice with lesser vision and proclaimed themselves the highest good. So, rather than destroy us along with our sin, He took our sin upon Himself and crucified it.

When Jesus breathed His last breath of humanity on that wondrous cross, our sins became completely deprived of the oxygen that gave them life. Moments after Jesus' hallowed cry, "*...It is finished...*" (John 19:30), God orchestrated a miraculous event from the heavens that would forever symbolize the cancellation of our sin and the invitation to an intimate, personal relationship with Him: *"At once the curtain in the temple was torn in two from top to bottom..." (Matthew 27:51, CEV).*

The curtain in the temple, the veil that separated God from people, was "torn in two," never to be patched or re-sewn or erected again. Tozer beautifully points out the relationship between our veils and the cross by saying:

> In human experience that veil is made of living spiritual tissue; it is composed of the sentient, quivering stuff of which our whole beings consist, and to touch it is to touch us where we feel pain. To tear it away is to injure us, to hurt us, and make us bleed. To say otherwise is to make the cross no cross and death

> no death at all. It is never fun to die. To rip through the dear and tender stuff of which life is made can never be anything but deeply painful. Yet that is what the cross did to Jesus and it is what the cross would do to every man to set him free.[26]

My firmly attached, patched, and repaired veils prevented me from engaging in the close, personal relationship to which the cross granted me access. Here I was, the girl on the bike who had fallen too many times to count, carried by a good Father into a realization I stumbled upon precisely because I *had* fallen. God was inviting me to stand in His presence as a bride before a groom, to lift my tattered veils and say yes to the acceptance He offered. For me to fully embrace his acceptance, I would need to grant him uninhibited access to every part—every wound.

Paul highlights the symbolism of the torn veil and its potential for life transformation in his letter to the Corinthian church:

> *But when one turns to the Lord, the veil is removed. Now the Lord is the Spirit and where the spirit of the Lord is, there is freedom. And we all, with unveiled face, beholding the glory of the Lord, are being transformed into the same image from one degree of glory to another. For this comes from the Lord who is the Spirit.*
>
> —2 Corinthians 3:16–18

I had read about this promise my whole life, yet never fully comprehended the severity of the sin lurking in me until that painful spring season. On the very day I felt most alienated from my heavenly Father, when I found myself in the middle of a situation I did not know how to climb out of, God let down a ladder—God came down to me. In His mercy, God opened my eyes to the only One who had the power to redeem my unspoken brokenness.

In his *Confessions*, Augustine recounts a similar revelation of his own:

> You resolved to restore my malformations, and with inward goads you roused me and made me restless until you were indisputably there before my inward sight. My swelling settled

> down under your unseen medical hand, and the disordered and darkened eyesight of my mind, when the stinging salve of wholesome sufferings was applied, was healing day by day.[27]

God sees through every veil, waiting with forbearance while His beloved children grope around in the darkness for the light God first conceived in us—a light that shone upon our unseen faces and marked us as His children. And only a good Father holds us steady while we kick against the goads meant to prod our stubborn souls into action. For He knows "*...this light momentary affliction is preparing for us an eternal weight of glory beyond all comparison*" (2 Corinthians 4:17).

I wish I could say that removing my veils was as instantaneous as God tearing the temple curtain that wondrous day. It was not. The process of tearing away my veils was more like what Tozer described—deeply painful and incredibly difficult. I had woven my veils into practices to cope with my wounds and sin. By relying on these veils rather than on God, I had turned them into stumbling blocks toward mature faith. But, when the reality of what Jesus truly accomplished on the cross landed in my soul, I saw, at last, the wretchedness of my disordered state—my sin. And, with new unencumbered sight, I saw the lies that, like thread, had woven together my veils.

I dealt with the veil of doubt first, though it was the last to be applied. I had strung it together with strands of false belief that God had not been good *to me*. I had sewn together this veil with the assumption that my heart was capable of deciphering truth. But the Lord tells us, through the prophet Jeremiah, that this is not so: "*The human heart is deceitful above all things, and desperately sick; who can understand it?*" (Jeremiah 17:9).

My heart told me that God's goodness hinged on my happiness, or worse, my happiness compared to my perception of others' happiness. The Lord is right to point out how desperately sick that is. To dismantle the lie stitched into this veil, I had to redefine good as the very essence of God, and therefore, anything and all things that brings God glory.

The scriptures affirm trust in a good God:

- "Oh give thanks to the Lord, for he is good; for his steadfast love endures forever!" (1 Chronicles 16:34)
- "Oh taste and see that the Lord is good! Blessed in the man who takes refuge in him!" (Psalm 34:8)
- "...No one is good except God alone." (Mark 10:18)
- "For how great is his goodness and how great his beauty..." (Zechariah 9:17)

Seeing good within this context removed me or my circumstances from the definition of good, thus, swinging wide the doors of opportunity for me to walk into *His goodness*.

It took me some time to adjust to my new set of lenses—the new perspective through which I attempted to see all things. Like someone who has just been prescribed reading glasses and does not yet reach for them out of automaticity, I had to be reminded to put on my spectacles before deciphering the words. God's goodness was all around, if only I had the right prescription. Eventually, with much repetition, and failure, and a firm resolve to never quit, I began to adopt God's definition of good as my own. It no longer took so much effort to identity and treasure it. I witnessed God's goodness in my husband's faithful, loving actions in the midst of my distress. I recognized God's goodness in the elderly gentleman at the grocery store, who told me my kids made the world a better place. I felt His goodness in the warm summer breeze, and in the comfort of sipping hot tea beside a blazing evening fire. Above all, I learned through the stories embedded in scripture and that He had *always been* good to me.

Perceiving life through a new perspective eventually allowed me to see the good, *His good*, in the midst of great uncertainty and physical pain. My incapacitated state may not have been able to bring glory to me, but, if I suffered well, it could possibly bring glory to Him. This truth acted like seam cutters, tearing away at the veil once adhered to my soul.

My unveiled condition granted me a stillness and peace I had never known in the midst of such turbulence. Like a captain's reassuring voice, the Spirit's truth pierced through the inclement weather. There may have been very little good in my physical situation, at the moment, but there was enough good in the cross to have my fill and pass the basket on.

The next veil I removed, the veil of avoidance, was the easiest to apply. However, I found it required much discipline to remove. For this veil boasts two sides: distraction and performance.

Our economy sustains itself with profits from gizmos designed to busy and divert our attention outwards. These days, we can go almost nowhere without being collared to a screen whose fine print upon ownership states that we be always within reach. The very electronics and apps designed under the guise of "making our lives easier" end up devouring our time and draining God's resources.

But God knew I could never heal by looking the other way. He knew I needed to tear my eyes away from the things of the world and fix them, instead, on Him. I needed God to teach me how to be silent with my own soul. I needed Him to hold my hand while I squirmed like a restless child in a waiting room.

God allowed my physical afflictions with divine foresight: "*For the Lord reproves him who he loves, as a father the son in whom he delights*" (Proverbs 3:12). I was learning, as Augustine did so long ago, of a sovereign Master unafraid to "fashion pain as a lesson and lambaste us to heal us and kill us so that we don't die away from you."[28]

This is a God who does not attempt to wrestle with us in the day, when our minds are preoccupied. No, He comes in the quiet, contemplative night of the soul. And if we cannot carve quiet into our numbered days, He may use His own means to quieten us.

In *The Spirit of the Disciplines,* Dallas Willard, quoting Louis Bouyer from *The Spirituality of the New Testament and the Fathers*, argues that solitude is one of the most essential spiritual disciplines, as exemplified through the life of Jesus Christ:

> But solitude, like all of the disciplines of the spirit, carries its risks. In solitude, we confront our own soul with its obscure forces and conflicts that escape our attention when we are interacting with others. Thus, "Solitude is a terrible trial, for it

> serves to crack open and burst apart the shell of our superficial securities. It opens out to us the unknown abyss that we all carry within us..." We can only survive solitude if we cling to Christ there. And yet what we find of him in that solitude enables us to return to society as free persons.[29]

I had been avoiding solitude, not as a means to avoid God, but as a means to avoid the depths of my own soul. Because once you know something, it can be hard to unknow it. And once you learn something, it cannot easily be unlearned. I've been told things about people that I wish I hadn't heard. Knowing creates a new reality for the knower. Perhaps, this is why we go to great lengths to avoid it.

To tear away the veil of avoidance, not only did I have to become acquainted with the new realities of my soul, I had to accept what I found.

Richard J. Foster, author of the beloved *Celebrations of Discipline,* writes, "Silence is one of the deepest Disciplines of the Spirit simply because it puts the stopper on all self-justification."[30] Without even knowing it, we callous our souls with our own manufactured explanations; we become numb to pain caused by our lives rubbing up against sin. But, in the silence, God sloughs off the callouses that have accumulated. And when He does, we can once again feel how much sin hurts us.

In my own contemplative silence, God revealed how I was using distraction to avoid His inward prodding. My phone, Netflix, and social media were more than harmless acquaintances; I had allowed them to kick down the door to my soul like thieves. They were rummaging through the drawers of my soul, stealing away precious bits of relational time with the only One who could make me well. The evidence of this break and enter was undeniable. I felt awkward and uncomfortable when I didn't pull out my phone while waiting for an appointment. I sometimes squandered valuable moments with my kids in my desire to capture the perfect photo for others to fawn over. I often rushed to get the kids to bed, or avoided my husband's clandestine invitations upstairs, to watch my favourite show, or two, or three.

I quietly decided to listen to God and then act, rather than self-justify. I cancelled Netflix and started to spend my evenings reading or in conversation. I went out and purposely left my phone at home to live my life more presently. I went off social media for a time to tame the desire to court others' good opinions of myself. I avoided any and all things that could potentially enslave me. After making those decisions, I have never felt freer. I did not usher in these changes to prove I was righteous or holy. On the contrary, I relinquished control over what I thought was permissible to the One infinitely more capable of pinpointing where my soul required discipline. Christ alone deserved my focused attention. Christ alone could accomplish the redemptive work that would heal my soul.

On the other side of my tattered veil of avoidance was performance. Working all things for my good, the Great Surgeon used my inability to *do* as a scalpel to cut away the belief that accomplishments would grant me worth. He wanted me to know I could not earn the love, peace, and joy I longed for—they were a passive gift of grace.

Removing this veil required laborious hours of ripping off what I had glued on. By pouring over God's word, which declared my inherent worth, I saw with lucid sight the ways in which I was striving for worth. The things I did for others were done as a security deposit, rather than a donation. If I did not receive thanks, I was offended. I knew little of a life lived hidden in Christ.

Throughout the days, weeks, and months that followed, I found myself circling around a proverbial wheel of feeling the need to strive, and then relinquishing that need in prayer. Daily, I dressed myself for battle with the full armour of God, and, daily, I wrestled this temptation to the ground. This was a monumental undertaking; I felt like I had been tasked with flattening the walls of Jericho. Even so, the God who remained true to Joshua kept His word to me and did not turn away from my broken and contrite spirit. He drew nearer still, sowing within me the indispensable truth that my value was in what Christ accomplished on my behalf, not in my own accomplishments or reputation. As this truth burrowed its roots in my soul, I found myself opening my hands to its implications—*I might never be physically healed or do what I had planned.* To live the life Christ was calling me into, I needed to lay down my definition of *great* and champion Christ's. The only way I could fully embrace my calling, whatever that may be, was if I loved God above all things.

Paradoxically, *once I chose* with all my heart, soul, and mind to treasure first the love of God, I found *inexpressible love* for Him.

In time, love for Him became my motivation for everything. The words of encouragement I spoke and acts of service I carried out, to an audience of One, only deepened the intimate, private relationship we now shared. In a way, I had to fail my way to finding the wondrous comfort and delight of living, hidden in Christ. Only after I'd finished picking up the pieces of my broken dreams did I see the beautiful mosaic He had been making.

The last veil I completely severed was the first I applied. Truth be told, there are still bits of this fabric soldered into our soul skin. The veil of control was the first to blanket humanity through Eve's selfish desire to be her own kind of god. This veil will always threaten to creep back over our lives until Jesus descends from His throne to raise the dead and rescue the living.

Until that time, we will always clamour after control, build our own kingdoms, and desire to be lesser gods. We will buck submission because we despise dependence and the feeling that we have been forsaken. The adversary wants more than anything for us to believe God is holding out on us, that He is keeping good things out of reach on purpose.

The truth to combat this lie is that God does not withhold anything good. Jesus Himself said, "*If you then, who are evil, know how to give good gifts to your children, how much more will your Father who is in heaven give good things to those who ask him!*" (Matthew 7:11).

God allows trials to teach us patience, self-control, trust, and how to surrender to His perfect plans. These fruits of the Spirit are all abundantly good.

As I twist the gold rings around my fingers and watch the decade-old diamonds glimmer in the sun, I remember the day I vowed before 200 spectators to marry Sam. That choice was exhilarating and powerful, but it was merely one public act meant to be re-affirmed by a lifetime of private actions.

Loving God with all my heart was simply the first choice of a million I needed to make, such as the way I stewarded my time. What I placed in front of my face, or pumped into my ears, or the thoughts I allowed into my mind would either help me keep this vow or dissuade me from keeping it. Each new day provided an opportunity to honour this vow by submitting my heart to His ways, or dishonour it by pursuing the idolatrous thrill of worshipping my ways above His. Christians are easily fooled into thinking loving God is an easy choice. God is wise to use scripture to remind us: "*Count it all joy... when you meet trails of various kinds, for you know that the testing of your faith produces steadfastness. And let steadfastness have its full effect, that you may be perfect and complete, lacking in nothing*" (James 1:2–4).

Testing my vow to God provided an opportunity to rediscover the One with whom I had begun a relationship in the first place. What I found was that He remained the same; it was I who changed. God the Father was as sure of my kinship as ever; it was I who secretly harboured doubts. Even still, as I allowed Him to woo me back to our first love, I came to see that belief can only truly exist when there is doubt, and a vow can only be truly kept when the option exists to not keep it.

Many writers much more talented than I have written fascinating books, such as *Bonhoeffer: Pastor, Martyr, Prophet, Spy* by Eric Metaxas, highlighting the cost of discipleship. When I read these books, I am amazed at how people not only survive but thrive under the gravest of circumstances when they are carried by hope. Paul beautifully articulates our greatest hope as disciples—Christ overcoming death and the corresponding hopes, of restoration of our decrepit bodies and the completion of His work in us—in 1 Corinthians 15:51–55:

> *Behold! I tell you a mystery. We shall not all sleep, but we shall all be changed, in a moment, in the twinkling of an eye, at the last trumpet. For the trumpet will sound, and the dead will be raised imperishable, and we shall be changed. For this perishable body must put on the imperishable, and this mortal body must put on immortality. When the perishable puts on the imperishable, and the mortal puts on immortality, then shall come to pass the saying that is written:*
>
> *"Death is swallowed up in victory."*

> *"O death, where is your victory?*
> *O death, where is your sting?"*

This passage is a beautiful reminder that I am but a sojourner on earth. The longings I felt for healing were God-breathed and destined to one day be fulfilled. I did not need to fear the physical pain I seemed shackled too or the urge to prove my worth. I could confidently rest in His promise of restoration and renewal.

Now that I had torn my veils by rediscovering Christ, I was free to embrace the brokenness that once lay hidden beneath the layers. I could look upon my soul—marked by wounds and sin—with reverence to the One who took the brunt of my blame upon His innocent shoulders. I could be a hope-filled kind of broken—a woman who acknowledges her great need for a saviour, yet despairs not because she believes in the miraculous healing awaiting her.

In *A Tale of Three Kings*, Gene Edwards describes the university in which God had me currently enrolled:

> God has a university. It's a small school. Few enrol: even fewer graduate. Very, very few indeed. God has this school because he does not have broken men and women. Instead, he has several other types of people. He has people who claim to have God's authority... and don't—people who claim to be broken... and aren't. And people who do have God's authority, but who are mad and unbroken. And he has, regretfully, a great mixture of everything in between. All of these he has in abundance, but broken men and women, hardly at all. In God's sacred school of submission and brokenness, why are there so few students? Because all students in this school must suffer much pain.

In my alma mater, I learned to submit myself, out of reverence, to Christ. Submission meant allowing God to use whatever means necessary to bring Him glory. In my instance, God used physical pain as a flashlight to expose the dark corners of my soul where trouble lurked. At first, the light was blinding; I was accustomed to and comfortable with fumbling around in the dark. Slowly, my eyes adjusted, and I could identify the unruly compartments of my soul. I could not decide to live a broken, submissive life just once—I needed to adopt it publicly.

The reason marriage and baptism are public declarations is simple: the spirit is willing, but the flesh is weak (Matthew 26:31). We are wayward creatures in desperate need of accountability. God was asking me to not only trust Him with my sin, but to invite trusted friends along this new-found journey of living in the light.

I began with a courageous phone call to a trusted friend. When she answered the phone, I sputtered out four words between sobs that finally broke through the dam of pride I had been constructing for so long.

"I am not okay."

I can recall the phone trembling in my hands and the immense relief that washed over me as the waters of my soul split through the rock, forging a new path—a new way of life.

I had always been the friend who had it all together. I was the rock that others depended on, except that I wasn't *really*. This is who I wanted others to see, but it wasn't the authentic me. The real me was full of holes and sin and in desperate need of a saviour. The real me needed friends who could love me in my dysfunctional state, lower me through the roof, and believe *that I could be healed*.

As I poured out my soul to my friend, I braced myself for the repercussions of this new-found vulnerability. After all these years of fraudulent living, I deserved a reprimand; I had earned, at the very least, stone cold silence on the other line. What my friend offered to me instead was pure, undeserved *grace*.

My friend's words were measured with assurance and dripping with authentic love.

"Kerri, thank you for your honesty," she said, and tears of relief poured out of me. "I've always wanted to get to know the real you. And to love that person. I am so very proud of you for taking this step and honoured that you chose me," she finished.

I had lived in constant fear that the real me, who struggled and barely limped along, was unlikable, when in actuality my dear friend had been patiently waiting for the real me to show up in our relationship for a long time.

God had been patiently waiting too—for classes to be out. He longed for me to embrace the broken plan that He had laid down at the foundations of the earth. The girl who fell off the bike was also the girl who poured over books for hours, wrote poetry, and studied lyric books on CDs like maps—in search of the treasure of a perfectly placed word. My good Father saw my fascination with prose, along with a heart that longed to know Him, and smiled to Himself at the plans He had prepared for me. The Author of life had already written my story—it was I who had forgotten the lines.

Responding to God's prompting, I attended a conference on tending the soul. Following a short session on listening to God for others, the speaker had us break off into groups of three to put into practice what we had just learned. I somewhat awkwardly made my way into a group with a woman about ten years younger than me and a woman forty years my senior. As per the speaker's request, this was our first encounter with one another. When it was my turn to be "listened for," the silence seemed to stretch on well past the designated three-to-five minutes. Clearly God had nothing to say. And then the older, remarkably gentle woman to my left broke the silence.

"Does a pen and paper mean anything to you?" she asked.

Something heavy shifted inside of me, almost like my interior furniture was being rearranged. All the pieces were the same, but the room looked entirely different.

"Yes," I managed weakly.

"Well," she said, "I want you to know I saw a pen—and there was a lot of ink left in that pen."

Amen.

Chapter Fifteen

the resurrection

You rose to set
the captives free.
You rose for all—
you rose for me.

THE ENTIRETY OF THE CHRISTIAN FAITH HINGES ON THE FACT THAT NOT ONLY did Jesus die, He rose again, forever defeating death. In John 5, we read about Jesus and his disciples returning to Jerusalem for one of the Jewish holidays. On their journey, they pass by a pool, known as Bethesda, where the blind, crippled, or paralyzed lie waiting for an opportunity to dip in the pool and be healed (John 5:3). The story zeroes in on one particular fellow who had been laying there for thirty-eight years, seemingly unable to move himself into the pool for healing. Jesus, moved with compassion, stops by this man and asks him a pointed question, "*...Do you want to be healed?*" (John 5:6).

Do you *want* to be healed? This question, I believe, is meant to pierce through the victim status we often feel in the midst of suffering. After we've survived the horrific explosion—when we wake up in the hospital bed with gruesome wounds to discover we still have a life to live—do we want to live that life at all?

There will come a time in almost all our lives when we are faced with these difficult questions: What does it mean to go on? What does it mean to get well?

What if getting well means nothing about our physical condition changing? What if it means more heart ache, more confession, more pain? What if getting well means forgiving the inexcusable? Or breaking off unhealthy relationships? Or painfully severing the ties of addiction—whether it be to distraction, or gossip, or food, or drink, or money? What if it means desiring more for ourselves than the temporary chapstick fix of fitting in? Rather than heal us, this cheap imitation balm quickly absorbs into our cracked skin, only leaving us desiring more. What if getting well means wading through floods and fires and terrible circumstances in order for God to reveal His mighty power?

These difficult questions ultimately lead back to the forbidden fruit that promised to save us from restraint. We were exhilarated to think that we could have *now* what God had been cultivating for forever. When we had the opportunity to choose, did we choose well? Or did Adam and Eve bite into the apple and let immediate gratification rule henceforth?

What does it take to to be more concerned about eternally-damned souls than perishing bodies? If we scaled that mountain in our minds, would we see with new clarity the outstretched hands set before us, bidding our crippled legs to stand? Would we grasp on tightly to the One who was busy stirring up the pool? The One who was calling us to submerge our whole bodies, not just our legs. The God of Abraham, Isaac, and Jacob, does not just call us to rise, He calls us all to run the race.

What happens next in John's rendition of this story is a beautiful picture of the rights we have as sons and daughters of the risen King. Even though the man peppers Jesus with excuses over his limited condition, Jesus says to him, "*...Get up, take up your bed, and walk*" (John 5:8).

The amazing truth embedded into the very fibre of our faith is that Jesus rose, and the invitation forever stands for us to rise too. We can rise up from whatever situation we find ourselves in, with rickety legs, and grab ahold of the hand extended towards us. Our condition does not matter. Christ has defeated death and, therefore, He has defeated every possible excuse. He calls us to simply, yet confidently, "stand up, and walk!" This is a call to obedience in Him, to a life void of self-trust and brimming with trust in a good, capable, holy, Father.

Praise be to God who resurrected a life I had committed to the grave. He breathed on dry bones and constructed a new me from the sedimentary dust. The life I had deemed worthless by the world's standards was of great value to God. He slowly opened my eyes to see that, if all I was capable of was praising Him, if my daily occupation was sitting at Jesus' feet as Mary did, it would be a life more worthy to Him than a thousand gold medals or successful titles.

Reaching up from my mat and taking God's hand brought me closer to His face than a lifetime of exchanging pleasantries. Putting the entirety of my weight on Him, however inconvenient and uncomfortable, offered me a fast-track to relational intimacy with the Father. God showed me a side of Him I could never know simply by being told. As such, my relationship with God evolved out of equal parts need and wonderment. I began to think of God as an entirely different being than me, rather than a heightened version of myself.

God's incommunicable traits[31] are what set Him entirely apart from us. For instance, God is unchangeable, while I change all the time. God is omnipresent, while I am stuck in one experience at a fixed point in time. My humanity will forever impede my total comprehension of God's deity. My understanding of the "whys" of life will never be fully realized with a limited mind. Trust in God ought not to be based on my own imperfect understanding, but on who He says He is, echoing the words of Solomon, "*Trust in the Lord with all your heart, and do not lean on your own understanding. In all your ways acknowledge him, and he will make straight your paths*" (Proverbs 3:5–6).

One particular night, in addition to the pain I had been experiencing, I awoke to frightening numbness along one side of my body. A series of stressful events over the past few months had me clinging to the edge of sanity. Within the span of two months, my son had broken his foot in a tobogganing accident, and my daughter had come down with pneumonia. I had been their rock during this time, but now I needed a rock of my own.

My husband drove me to the emergency room, despite his internal dialogue concluding that I was fine. I did not feel fine, yet something within me sensed God was at work. And He was. The Great Physician was about to give me a lesson in how He sometimes uses bodies we don't want, and experiences we would never choose, to heal the only part of us that lasts forever—our souls.

As I sat across from the ER doctor, I saw the concern in his intelligent eyes. I could tell by his furrowed brow that he thought there was something wrong with me. But after the unveiling, this came as no surprise. I already knew something was wrong.

As I sat in the loose-fitting nightgown that felt like my life—never fitting the way I imagined it should—I sobbed. In that moment, I realized something had powerfully shifted inside of me. My tears were not tears of fear, they were tears of release. I didn't know what the doctor would say, or why I was experiencing a loss of sensation, but I knew the promises of the Rock on which I was standing.

The doctor turned and looked at me inquisitively, before he spoke these words. "Kerri, has your doctor talked to you about the possibility of your symptoms being related to MS? I think it's something we need to pursue. I have ordered an MRI to test for it."

When he finished his sentence, I replayed a conversation with my family doctor from the last time I went to see him about my pain. He had drawn a similar conclusion and fear had risen like the mercury ball in summer. This time, after hearing the same words, I felt different—sad, but not afraid.

I returned home and contacted our small group from church immediately. I told them that my understanding, based on what the doctor said, was that MS is detected by an MRI, revealing specific lesions on the brain that relate to areas of the body where symptoms are being experienced. No lesions = no MS. We began to pray specifically that my MRI would be clear and show no signs of lesions. During the three weeks I had to wait for the MRI and the results, I had trouble sleeping, but the restlessness felt different than it had before, like I was somehow being held inside of the uncertainty instead of pressed down by it. During the odd hours awake, I prayed because it helped. It seemed God was providing the opportunity our relationship needed, albeit in the middle of the night, to court. We took turns asking questions across the table.

What had brought me here?

Who was this Christ and could He be trusted?

Did I put my hope in my circumstances?

What did for better or worse really mean?

Four weeks later, I found myself sitting in the neurologist's office, tapping my feet on the concrete floors. After what seemed like hours, a tall black man entered the room. When he extended his hand to introduce himself, I was bathed in the confidence he exuded. He opened my file and read to me the answer we had fervently prayed for—I did not have MS! But, although the MRI results brought much joy, my body and soul groaned in unison for answers.

After my visit to the emergency room, I had started working with a psychologist to determine if anxiety or depression was causing some of my physical symptoms. For the first time in my life, I was able and willing to accept help. I no longer feared what I didn't know. My relationship with the Father was teaching me a posture of curiosity rather than consternation. In working with my psychologist and spending time silent before God, I was uncovering things I had veiled for so long—I struggled with control. I was anxious. I cared deeply what others thought of me. I had been hurt by the words and actions of friends and family in my past. I was enamoured with success. The wounds and sin God exposed no longer seemed ominous. I did not reach for the familiarity of the veils. Instead, I could look at my wounds in all their complexities and admire the protective scab the Healer's truth had begun to form over them.

As I sat in the neurologist office, I had a sudden, irresistible urge to chuckle. Fear had officially vacated the room. God's peace that surpasses all understanding washed over me instead.

After a battery of questions and a few tests, he looked at me and said, "I know what it is that has been causing your physical problems."

Instantly, my heart raced and sweat rose up in my palms like water from a deep well. I had prepared myself for everything except a concrete answer.

"You have cervical dystonia," he forged on, obviously unaware of the warning sirens blaring on my insides.

"Basically, your brain resists the signal to turn your head left, causing your muscles to over tone on one side." His large hands stretched out toward my neck and I winced at their abrupt assertions.

"See here?" He brushed the left side of my neck lightly. "It is much thicker; it is over toned."

He pulled his hands back and studied me intently before looking for other signs of this condition on my hands and feet. Sure enough, the evidence was there. The things He pointed out were rather insignificant, yet, when documented by his well-trained eye, the whole picture came into focus—I had the condition of which he spoke.

At first, I was in shock. I could hardly believe that the physical discomfort I had been experiencing had a name. It took me a while to fully appreciate how miraculous the appointment had been in the first place. The only reason I was here, sitting in this office, with this answer was because this neurologist happened to know my family doctor, and he happened to specialize in this condition. I had even showed up to my appointment a day early to find out that the person who was supposed to come at that time never showed up!

When I was twelve, I had braces slapped across my crooked smile. Despite being on almost three years, the orthodontist could not seem to bring my jaw into perfect alignment. Frustrated with my lack of progress, the orthodontist took the braces off. Oh the irony of this situation now. My jaw would not conform to the braces because it *could* not. My brain would not allow it. This echoed the pursuit of my inner life. I was made in the image of God, and yet I was trying to bend my identity to the world, wondering why it never seemed to perfectly align.

The doctor advised me not to look up this condition on the internet because it would "scare the hell out of me." Although his chilling words pricked my ears, I was not afraid. I felt confident and secure in my *good* Father's plan for me. The doctor then provided for me an analogy for my newfound diagnosis.

"Think of it like this," he said. "There is an angel on your right shoulder bidding to you to look right—that's the way your brain wants you to look. And there is a devil on your left shoulder, tempting you to look left, but it is never in your best interest to look left. When you look left it will cost you something. Remember that."

Looking back, I can't help but smile at God's thumbprint of truth in the doctor's words. The truth is, we all need to make the choice to look right or left—to the proverbial angel or devil on our shoulders. Our gracious Father put us in the garden with two options, all the while knowing our tendency to turn left, whatever the cost, is strong. Mainstream culture provides little resistance against swimming towards health, wealth, and prosperity. I was learning the greatest blessings can seem, at the time, like barricades. This physical condition, which had put life as I knew it on hold, was calling my attention back to the direction I was turning my soul.

Walking out of the office, I felt trapped inside the tunnel of my own thoughts, which were splitting through my centre at blazing speed. I could not stop them or command them in any way; I was merely the shaft they must pass through.

Suddenly, the train of thought racing through my mind screeched to a halt on one particular realization, a gift from my heavenly Father: this condition that lay undiagnosed beneath physical pain and confusion had been woven into my DNA in the darkness of my mother's womb when the only One who saw my face was God. And that same God had stared fondly upon His new creation, crafted with great ingenuity for a particular purpose, and smiled. For what God makes is always *good*—I am no exception.

Labels, diagnoses, and medical conditions are all attempts at categorizing God's creations. We are so easily deceived into thinking that, because some of us are different than others, then some of us were made less good. That is a deceptive lie that seeks only to steal, kill, and destroy (John 10:10). From the moment of conception, no matter the human DNA that flows through our tiny vessels, or gene mutation we develop in utero, or acquired illness that strikes our fragile bodies—we have been stamped with the image of God. We are but reflections, tiny snippets of a glorious light, that have been made to illuminate one face: His. And no matter how the world measures us, or attempts to define us, or cuts us down, one thing is for certain—God smiled when He made us.

As I got into my car that day, I couldn't help but tilt my head to the right, up to the heavens and smile back at the face that first saw me and called me good. With a newly discovered blessed assurance, I trusted in my inherent goodness because God had revealed to me, as he did to St. Augustine so very long ago, that no soul was *"able to conceive of anything better than thee, who art the highest and best good."*[32] And if that Good calls me good, it is very safe to say I am indeed, good.

Chapter Sixteen

by his wounds, i am healed

Standing still in disbelief,
my head is hanging low.
My hope has surely dissipated
with life's last final blow.

You seek me out and meet my gaze,
Your hands outstretched in view,
You beckon me, a closer look
to touch where nails tore through.

Your life snuffed out most willingly.
My blinded eyes now see
the wounds You wore on my behalf—
memorials of love for me.

Perhaps the most amazing truth about our faith is that we Christ followers, a deeply wounded people, get to be whole-heartedly acknowledged and intimately known by a wounded Christ. Our beloved saviour, whose body was split open and blood was spilled, underwent the most public display of brokenness the world has ever seen. Not only did He break, the King of the world chose to be broken. We can be confident of this because, the night before His death, when Jesus left His disciples to pray in the garden of Gethsemane, He experienced what the medical community now describes as hematidrosis (bloody sweat). Jesus was under such great emotional stress over what was about to happen to Him that tiny capillaries in His sweat glands burst open, mixing blood with his sweat. The only possible explanation for this bodily manifestation of stress was that He knew what was to come. He drank His cup wholly distraught and *completely submitted to the Father's will.* Jesus set a new bar for the category of the wrongly convicted and accepted His fate without so much as an utterance of foul speech. As the prophet Isaiah says: "*He was oppressed, and he was afflicted, yet he opened not his mouth; like a lamb that is led to the slaughter, and like a sheep that before its shearers is silent, he opened not his mouth*" (Isaiah 53:7).

These first fissures erupting beneath His skin were only the beginning of the torture Jesus chose to endure on our behalf. The Bible describes, rather mildly, the events following Jesus' capture, when He was struck across the face, blind-folded, mocked, battered, bruised, beaten, dehydrated, and forced to carry an 110-pound cross from the prison, up a hill to the place He was to be executed.

Death by crucifixion in Jesus' day was the most horrific death one could possibly endure. In our protected society, so far removed from this type of torturous death, it is easy to skip over the significance of it, the magnitude of sacrifice His death required. We often invite sin into our lives and live with less mercy when, as Dallas Willard articulates, "we have not looked closely at the lengths to which God had to go to reach *us*. We have not learned to live always and thankfully in the cross's shadow."[33]

In *The Case for Christ*, Lee Strobel interviews doctor and scholar Alexander Metherell to gain a more accurate perception of pain involved in crucifixion:

> The pain was absolutely unbearable.... In fact, it was literally beyond words to describe; they had to invent a new word: *excruciating*. Literally, *excruciating* means "out of the cross." Think of that: they needed to create a new word, because there was nothing in the language that could describe the intense anguish caused during the crucifixion.[34]

Contemplating Jesus' physical death may provide a doorway through which our simple minds can enter into understanding the cost of the crucifixion. With the weight of our sin crushing His son, God chose to abandon the part of a trinity that has existed in community for all of time. There is no relational bond that has ever been stronger and, therefore, no bond more excruciating to break. This alone unequivocally proves the height and depth of His love for us (Romans 8:38).

The Bible does not describe the emotional devastation Jesus felt as he died—Luke simply records, "*Then Jesus, calling out with a loud voice, said, 'Father, into your hands I command my spirit!' And having said this He breathed his last*" (Luke 23:46). Jesus died in our place, needing no recognition for the magnitude of His sacrifice. Hanging on the cross, He proved once and for all His commitment to His vows. If someone was going to leave the relationship it would be us, not Him.

God could have orchestrated any type of death, yet he allowed, perhaps even chose, death by crucifixion to exemplify the very act of breaking Jesus' physical body so that we would never be able to dispute what happened. Christ broke. And this paved the way for all those enrolled in God's sacred school of submission to henceforth equate brokenness with holiness.

Since the beginning of time, God has scattered examples of holy brokenness all over His creation. Farmers plough the hard earth to plant seeds; forests burn to rid themselves of disease and break open their resin-sealed cones; egg shells crack to unveil new life; the amniotic sac ruptures and the perineum tears to bring forth that first hallowed cry; clams are shucked; nuts are cracked—these examples of holy breaking are everywhere you look. Perhaps humans need to see physical breaking with our eyes and touch it with our hands on a daily basis in order to understand that brokenness is a part of God's redeeming plan. Too often, we spend time wondering how, despite brokenness, our lives can continue on, instead of wondering how our lives are propelled forward *because* of it.

Jesus' death on the cross is an invitation to embrace even our most unspoken brokenness, knowing that God has already orchestrated a plan that will bring glory to Him. This is great news for those of us who find ourselves on the broken road. Although this road may begin with the realization that we are in great need, it ends with the conclusion that Mary, Peter, Paul, and countless others came to—He is an all sufficient supplier. We can hold to this belief in good company.

Perhaps one of the most beautiful acts of holy brokenness by a person in the New Testament is when an unnamed, sinful woman cracks an alabaster jar of perfume to anoint Jesus' feet.

Luke records the story of Jesus joining a Pharisee for a meal. While Jesus and the Pharisee recline at the table, a customary way of eating at the time, a woman catches wind of Jesus' location and eagerly bursts onto the scene—clearly uninvited. The passage of scripture used to introduce this new character describes her as "*...a woman of the city, who was a sinner...*" (Luke 7:37).

Perhaps aware of the intrusiveness of the situation, the woman does not come empty-handed—she brings a gift, but not for the host. Her gift is for the guest. Wasting no time, the woman falls to Jesus' feet. She wets and washes them using nothing other than the very essence of herself, her tears and her hair. Then, she breaks open what was likely her most valuable earthly possession to pour over Jesus' feet. Veils torn, this woman willingly accepts her label as "sinner" and holds Jesus up in the highest regard, humbling herself by washing His feet—a job reserved for only the lowliest of servants. Later on, Jesus himself models this very action as the posture of a true disciple, yet it seems the genuine and contrite heart of a believer needs no teaching on the subject.

The unsettled thoughts of the Pharisee hosting the party are so loud, they slice through the tension in the story first. He says to himself "*...if this man were a prophet, he would have known who and what sort of woman this is who is touching him, for a she is a sinner*" (Luke 7:39).

Jesus chooses to reply with a story that attempts, like always, to remove the scales from unbelieving eyes, unveiling truth and holding up sincerity as the treasure for which we should be willing to risk our lives.

The parable He unpacks is about a money lender and two debtors. The first debtor owes much money and the second only owes a little. Neither debtors are able to pay the moneylender, who, in an act of mercy, decides to cancel both debts.

Jesus then turns to the Pharisee, the one who is the target of this arrow of truth, and probes, "*...Now which of them will love him more?*" (John 7:42).

In this statement, Jesus expresses his concern with the posture of our hearts above all else. He wants to know what we treasure, what our gazed is fixed upon, who our identity is established in: "*For where your treasure is, there your heart will be also*" (Matthew 6:21).

When the Pharisee saw the sinful woman touching Jesus, it challenged his hierarchical worldview. The Pharisee treasured his position and power more than the One it stood for. He treasured the oil flowing out of the jar more than the feet of the One it anointed. He was blind to his true identity, and therefore, veiled to the wondrous beauty of Christ.

In stark contrast, when the woman laid eyes on Jesus, she saw the supplier of her one true need. She confidently unveiled her brokenness because this Redeemer possessed the ability to blot out every sin. And the nameless, sinful woman was right. Her extravagant act of worship garnered a lavish response from Jesus meant to spur us all toward humility and repentance. Jesus said to her, "*Your faith has saved you; go in peace*" (Luke 7:50).

Unbeknownst to me, God had used my trials and physical diagnosis to unveil my true identity. I was not the Pharisee I sometimes acted like. Here, hidden in the shadow of His wings, I mustered the courage to stare straight into the mirror I had avoided for so long. This time, the reflection did not take me by surprise—there I was, the sinful woman, tears streaking down my face and humbly on my knees. As I wet my hair to anoint the feet of my saviour, I saw with unrestricted vision the beauty of the One who hung upon the cross—exhausted, beaten down, bruised, and cracked open, pouring out pure uninhibited love for me.

Jesus was no longer someone I had to host and impress with my position. He was someone who knew my sinful nature and yet loved me enough to make and execute a plan to rescue me. One who took pain upon Himself to render the temple veil torn, validating the pain I would have to go through to tear my own.

The realization of my true identity had me ready to crack my alabaster plans to pieces, if only in some small way to express my gratitude over what He had done. Even still, the One whose feet I was preparing to anoint, in turn, began to pour His ointment of grace over me. I was soon drenched in the fragrant oil of surrender to a good and gracious God.

The Bible reveals a particular pattern time and time again, yet somehow in all my years as a Christian I had missed it: an exile, a desert season, a time of testing, followed by a promise and a rescue. We have to get through the desert to reach the promised land; we have to suffer on a cross to bring healing to the world. It's a paradox that few ever truly grasp and, yet, it is precisely the way His backwards kingdom operates. This is why so many have ears but are deaf, and have eyes but are blind, to the treasure that is just within their reach (Mark 8:18).

If I truly wanted to be made well, I had to be willing to bring my alabaster jar to Jesus' feet, trusting that He came to break for me, a sinful woman. The holy son of God, birthed in a stable, grew into a man with feet braced for shards. He paved the broken way. Knowing this, we can be confident that every tear, every sleepless night, every groan of longing, every cry of pain is the perfumed offering of dreams cracked open and autonomy spilled out. For not one ounce of our suffering, like perfume poured over His precious feet, will He waste.

The sinful woman knew with quiet, devout confidence that a life poured out for the sake of Christ was more gain to her than a life spent clinging to clay. God called me into this same type of reckless faith by schooling me into submission with earthly failure. He knew, no matter at what height I set the bar of achievement, I would never jump high enough to clear it. Claiming brokenness as a sinful woman and submitting my life, like Christ, formed the stinging salve by which my wounds were finally healed. The Psalmist outlines the prerequisite for healing in this way: "*He heals the brokenhearted, and binds up their wounds*" (Psalm 147:3).

In my dark night of the soul, a term coined by St. John of the Cross, I believed that God abandoned me. In actuality, God was using my brokenness as a means to rediscover what Christ accomplished for me on the cross. My wounded soul and subsequent sin—doubt, need for control, exalting success—could be healed and forgiven so that I could be transformed into someone more like Christ, someone who bore scars.

But what exactly did it mean to heal? How did I know it was being accomplished? I found healing, for me, to be two-fold: action and rest, the same tension that exists in scripture in the way Jesus conducted Himself.

The action involved laborious work to dig myself out of the ruts I had spun my tires into. My new physical diagnosis required me to train my head to function differently because looking left now came at a cost—tension, pain, and possibly more problems with my spine as I age. Not looking left, spiritually, involved constant awareness of the posture of my soul.

I attempted to explain my physical diagnosis to my children by letting them know that I needed them to sit on my right side when reading and talking to me. A twinkle of mischief crossed my worker man's eyes. Before I could say anything else, he was on my left side, chirping like a parakeet so his sister would know she should laugh, "Can you see me Mom, can you see me?" I, too, partook in the humour and absurdity of this condition by chuckling alongside them. Yet, in the same breath, I could not ignore the powerful metaphor God had orchestrated in my physical body to aid in my understanding of the soul.

Without a doubt, my disordered eating, need for control, fear, and striving had stemmed from looking left, to the world. And, like my neurologist, the Great Physician knew every glance in the wrong direction came with a cost. What then would it take to stop my soul from looking left? I needed to be reminded why I should choose to look right. Who exactly is the One upon whom my eyes should be fixed? I rediscovered, through scripture, that He is:

My rock, fortress, and deliverer (Psalm 18:2)
A true friend who withholds nothing (John 15:15)
Unquestionably faithful (1 Corinthians 10:13)
Patient (2 Peter 3:9)
Giving (James 1:17)
One who fulfills promises (Numbers 23:19)
Just (Psalm 50:6)
Present (Joshua 1:9)
Compassionate (Micah 7:19)

Loving (1 John 4:8)
Victorious (Deuteronomy 20:4)

The more I practised holding each thought captive before turning my head right, the more natural it became. After all, I was not a victim of my thoughts—I was the perpetrator of them. Each thought granted me the opportunity not to overvalue my life on earth at the expense of undervaluing eternity. The book of James has these wise words to corroborate this truth:

> *Come now, you who say, "Today or tomorrow we will go into such and such a town and spend a year there and trade and make a profit"—yet you do not know what tomorrow will bring. What is your life? For you are a mist that appears for a little time and then vanishes. Instead you ought to say, "If the Lord wills, we will live and do this or that."*
>
> —James 4:13–15

Basing my thoughts and emotions on mist and placing my hope in plans was foolish and short-sighted. God was teaching me to take the long view of life, one that surpassed death and lived on into eternity. Behind my veils, I had hidden a treasure chest of my earthly accolades. I was not heeding Jesus' words of warning about the moth, the rust, and the thieves, another powerful metaphor for the fate of our worldly wealth. It simply does not last. The reality of our society is that some people never accept this truth. And when their earthly shells are buried six feet under the wealth they amassed, it will be too late. Not so for the children of God who open their ears to His life-altering advice. Now is not forever. Our pain—however intense and crippling it may seem—is but a fleeting moment in the grand expanse of eternity. When the obituary has been read and the guest book signed, we will have only just begun. And what a waste it will be if we squander our time on the introduction and miss the whole story.

Instead, let's allow the words of the prophet Isaiah to dictate how we navigate our necessary, earthly course:

Have you not known? Have you not heard?
The Lord is the everlasting God,
the Creator of the ends of the earth.
He does not faint or grow weary;
his understanding is unsearchable.
He gives power to the faint,
and to him who has no might he increases strength.
Even youths shall faint and be weary,
and young men shall fall exhausted;
but they who wait for the Lord shall renew their strength;
they shall mount up with wings like eagles;
they shall run and not be weary;
they shall walk and not faint.

—Isaiah 40:28–31

After training my physical body and spiritual soul to keep their eyes to the right, what came next in my healing was most welcomed *rest*. The hallmark of any wonderful relationship is being able to sit comfortably in silence. Replacing awkwardness with love and peace is a sure sign that the relationship has arrived.

God drew near to me in my brokenness by extending His hand to welcome me into a divine dance of relational intimacy—the only requirement was to rest in His confident embrace. Barbara Brown Taylor describes this sort of divine visit in these words:

> I have courted the Beloved long enough to know it is like coming home after a long time away; it is like being held by someone with all the time in the world; it is like remembering a dream that opens a door. Earlier in my life I wanted more specificity than that. I wanted a divine parent who would give me direct answers, clear guidance, specific tasks. Now that I have accepted responsibility for supplying those things myself, it is enough to step away from them from time to time, resting in the presence of the Beloved who accepts all answers, covers all direction, finishes all tasks.[35]

I recall a difficult day, shortly after my diagnosis, in which my mind struggled to respond to the demands of motherhood. I could not wait for quiet time to roll around. Quiet time is the designated time in my day when the children are expected to occupy themselves while I participate in the all-important task of resting my mind. Sometimes I read my Bible, sometimes I pray, and sometimes I lie silently, listening to the trickling down of my own thoughts. Once my body had eased itself into my familiar divot in the couch, the overwhelming presence of God swept over me—a divine visit. For two minutes, or five, or maybe half an hour, all awareness of time eluded me, and all I did was cry. I felt as if my husband were in the room holding me between sobs, His presence was that comforting. I named fear after fear while the tears spilled out. I felt my wounds, inflamed by feelings of abandonment, diminish and close that day. God never left. I could lay down my head, tired and weary from searching for meaning in the world, to rest.

Each and every time I accept the open invitation to rest in His confident embrace, something remarkable and miraculous happens—the wounds close in.

It's a warm summer day, the kind that is stretched on by steaming cups of coffee and children scampering about in breakfast-stained pyjamas. We've just returned from another camping trip and, after living in each other's space, we're used to being close, familiar skin rubbing up against familiar skin.

My phone lights up with a message from a friend; they've just given birth to their third child—a beautiful daughter, a fruit of the womb, a blessed inheritance, an arrow for their quiver. Three healthy children gifted to a healthy, able-bodied mom. My fingers fumble across the puckered edges of the scar that signifies the healing of my once-marred soul. The hallow places have been filled and sealed. I keep brushing across the edges where the wound once was, trying to figure out what emotions linger there—what is my new truth? I lower my basin into the well of my soul to see what emotion surfaces with it. Joy!

Almost reflexively, I thank God for the way He has graciously restored function to a part of me I once deemed beyond repair.

I respond to her message with sincere words poured out from a soul that now bears a mark—pink, shiny, and raised like a scar.

I stand from my chair, phone in hand, and search for my husband to share with him God's victory lived out in me. Only God and my husband know the battle that it's been, how invasive the surgery and the long road of recovery that followed. I find him tucked away in our oversized couch with a lap full of our two children, mouthing child-sized syllables. My words slip out on the heels of so much joy that I've lost control of where they land.

"Our friend, Kim, they had their third baby, it's a girl." I pause, just to make sure the words I am about to utter are genuine and that they are truth.

Yes—this feels authentic—this feels true.

"I'm so happy for them. Really happy."

I can't explain the joy I feel, almost as if this child were my own precious gift, an extension of a larger family I will always and forever belong to. That I can experience joy at God giving to another what He withheld from me is a monument proclaiming that healing the soul is not only possible, it is lasting, it is real, and one day it will be forever.

In similar soul fashion, now, when I make my nightly tread down the well-worn paths of my neighbourhood, shaded by centuries-old trees and come across a woman with a stride that outmatches mine, I quietly give thanks to God for her ability. I whisper a blessing under my breath for continued health, for the ability to run without pain. And miraculously, I mean every word of it. The same girl who dreamed of wearing a Canadian flag for her country, with a coach who first recognized her innate talent and believed she could; the girl who was able to push herself beyond all reasonable limits; the one who would have never quit trying if not for the ache of having her bones break under the weight of a great ambition—this girl has picked up the pieces of her shattered tear-stained dreams and seen their imperfectly perfect shimmer.

And finally, the words that first dug malicious claws into soul flesh, that ones that I allowed to injure me again and again, have been drowned out by Another's song I am fearfully and wonderfully made (Psalm 139:14). Each time, the familiar tune of a birthday celebration hangs over the person of honour, like balloons and the cake is made, lit, cut, and finally served—I savour each bite free from thoughts of captivity that once entangled my mind in their thorny vines. True beauty is found in a surrendered soul. This truth has freed me from the eating disorder that once shackled me.

Although the wounds that once marred my soul have been healed, I have not yet healed from my physical condition. Stumbling after the persistent widow's faith (Luke 18), as long as I still suffer, I will continue to ask God for complete physical healing. However, my faith in a good and able God is not contingent on my physical healing or what He does for me here on earth.

Yes, I have faith in a God who is more than capable of healing any infirmity. Even still, in keeping with the tensions held in scripture, I must also have faith in His wisdom and restraint. I can be confident in God's promise to one day heal me, while trusting He is not bound to my timeline. Faith like this, that's full of tension, provides the elasticity for God to be the full expanse of who He is.

Jesus addresses this tension in one of the last conversations with His beloved follower, Peter, under whose leadership the Church flourished. Near the end of the book of John, Peter asks Jesus about the apostle John's mission, to which Jesus responds with a simple yet profound statement—"*...you, follow me!*" (John 21:22).

I must take to heart Jesus' instructions to Peter, believing that the mission and circumstances in which God has placed me are unique to His plan for *me*. Jesus asks for trust and obedience. He does not offer an explanation.

I have learned that I can joyfully obey Jesus in this invitation to follow His plan for my life, regardless of my present circumstance, because of what He has already accomplished. Jesus did not send His followers out on mission without firmly planting the seed of hope in their hearts. He proved His trustworthiness first, and obedience naturally followed.

Peter, the one who doubted, and denied, and finally surrendered to Christ's purposes, understood the great depth behind the words, "*...By his wounds you have been healed*" (1 Peter 2:24). This healing Peter references does not make a world riddled with sin to be without consequence, it does not make catastrophic events un-catastrophic, and it does not give anyone the permission to begin a sentence to a neighbour who has lost a family member with "at least..."

This type of healing is personal and relational, and yet produces an outcome that is miraculously the same in us all. For some, the process may be long and hard fought, it may involve forgiving oneself or another, it may involve changing one's life, or it may involve patience in prayer. For others, the healing may be instantaneous. One moment of living in the shadow of the cross may be enough to live in step with the Spirit—to live whole. We must never judge a person's journey or position on their journey toward soul healing, for only the Father knows the precise time and attention it will take for each of His individual creations to heal. We can, however, be sure of one thing: when the wound closes from the inside out, there will be proof. The collision with God's grace and love will leave us permanently altered with a scar, forever proclaiming to a wounded world the healing balm called Christ—available to any and all who call upon His name.

In the same way the prodigal son was changed through his repentance, no longer viewing His Father as a dispenser of good things but as inherently good—we too will think different thoughts that cause us to lead different lives once we have been healed. John 15:5 proclaims this truth: "*I am the vine; you are the branches. Whoever abides in me and I in him, he it is that bears much fruit...*"

I have learned through my own miraculous soul healing that fruit means knowing deeply the love of my Father. Fruit means joy in my own circumstance and the circumstances of others. Fruit means peace while enduring hard times. Fruit means patience in the midst of affliction, bodily or spiritually. Fruit means gentleness in the way I treat other wounded individuals. Fruit means self control over what I watch, read, listen to, say, and all the other ways I steward the twenty-four hours I am gifted each day. And praise be to the risen Lord that no one, not even the adversary, will ever be able to stop the vine from producing all this holy ripened fruit in us.

In the powerful, prophetic words of Annie J. Flint:

He giveth more grace when the burdens grow greater,
He sendeth more strength when the labors increase;
To added afflictions He addeth His mercy,
To multiplied trials, His multiplied peace.

When we have exhausted our store of endurance,
When our strength has failed ere the day is half done,
When we reach the end of our hoarded resources
Our Father's full giving is only begun.

Fear not that thy need shall exceed His provision,
Our God ever yearns His resources to share;
Lean hard on the arm everlasting, availing;
The Father both thee and thy load will upbear.

His love has no limits, His grace has no measure,
His power no boundary known unto men;
For out of His infinite riches in Jesus
He giveth, and giveth, and giveth again.[36]

The words of this book I'm writing sprouted like blossoms out of a healed soul. I am one with the leper in Galilee, who Jesus made well. You see, even though Jesus said, "*...See that you say nothing to anyone, but go show yourself to the priest and offer for your cleansing what Moses commanded for a proof to them*" (Mark 1:44), the cleansed leper spread the news throughout the entire town. Because no matter the powers of hell or schemes of man, news this good simply cannot be restrained.

Chapter Seventeen

jesus bore scars

What is a scar?
A mark? A brand?
Is it altered skin
or an outstretched hand?

Does it connect two hearts?
Does it sew a thread?
Does it bind up pain?
Does it erase all dread?

A scar means change,
For Him, for me.
It's a brilliant seal
declaring victory.

I BEAR MANY SCARS. THERE ARE THE PHYSICAL SCARS, SUCH AS THE ONE ON MY knee from when I fell off my bike, or the one on my wrist from when I held my arm over a steaming kettle reaching for a paper towel, or the ones that resemble zebra stripes from my abdomen stretching to accommodate the miracle of new life. Then, there are the scores of hidden scars that zigzag across my soul like a piece of abstract art, one of a kind, curated by the Father.

Kintsugi is a traditional Japanese art form in which broken ceramics are repaired with a precious metal, such as liquid silver or gold: "By repairing broken ceramics it's possible to give a new lease on life to the pottery that becomes even more refined thanks to its 'scars.' The Japanese art of kintsugi teaches that broken objects are not something to hide but to display with pride."[37] This can be a difficult art form to appreciate in a world in which flawless finishes are often exalted. Cracks are uncomfortable to look at because we've been conditioned to wince at the sight of broken things.

Embracing the artistry in brokenness glorifies the One who broke first for us. Like kintsugi, the cracks in my soul had been beautifully filled in and painted over by the Father's most precious materials—grace and love. My soul could be lovingly gazed upon as a one-of-a-kind masterpiece, finished and curated by the Father. The scars are what give my soul inherent value, for they serve as the very evidence of His divine presence and healing.

I sit at breakfast with my three-year-old daughter. She's eating toast, globs of peanut butter gathering at the corners of her silly grin. After taking a big swig of her milk, a moustached mouth turns to me and speaks the question that's been clouding her innocent eyes, "Mom, does it hurt to have a baby?"

I stare lovingly at the tiny creature before me, who now miraculously speaks in full sentences, recounting in my mind the two unbelievably painful labours I've experienced. The first almost killed me. I laboured for hours without end and then pushed for hours without end until they were forced to split my tender flesh to slide the burgeoning life out of me.

My second was not as traumatic, but I chose, with a will passed down to me by my father, to do it without drugs. I wanted to be initiated into motherhood knowing the cost. I wanted to feel every pulsating contraction and excruciating push because I knew deep within that this would be the easy part.

I lift up my shirt slightly to show my daughter the evidence of her humble beginning, sheltered within my womb. The stretch marks that pucker my belly are evidence of the way motherhood altered me physically and emotionally, forever. Because the very best things in life do not leave us untouched.

Paul E. Miller puts it this way: "We don't love someone without it changing us. This is just the nature of love that reflects the heart of God. Because God's love is unchanging, the second person of the Trinity, Jesus of Nazareth, now has a scarred body. The Trinity is different because of love."[38]

When Christ rose, when His old self died and came back to life in a heavenly body, a resurrected-free-from-pain existence, He did so bearing scars. Christ was the first to enter into a new existence, life after death, and yet His perfect body is perfectly marred with scars. What a surprising paradox!

What purpose could permanently-altered flesh possibly serve in a risen existence? What is altogether lovely and beautiful about seared skin? How could Jesus' imperfection be viewed by God as divine perfection? Surely God could have erased the marks of defeat from His Son's holy skin. That is, unless, His scars are not signs of defeat at all. Perhaps God views Jesus' scars as sacred evidence of His love colliding with lives: holy impact, followed by catastrophic breaking, and then, most importantly, a redemptive healing that leaves Jesus' hands forever changed—for us.

When my son held out that Lego cross to me on my soul's dark night, his tiny hands operated as extensions of the One who raised him up and sent him out on the same divine mission we all share—to show others the road home. Because, the truth is, sometimes we lose our way. I know I did. But the good news is that we have a God who has greatly concerned Himself with seeking out the lost.

Throughout the Old Testament, time and time again, God is described as a Good Shepherd who cares for His sheep. Jesus expands upon this characteristic by telling a story about a lost sheep. He goes so far as to say that the shepherd is so concerned about finding the one lost sheep that he leaves the ninety-nine. That's an incredible risk. But, for the shepherd, it is also absolutely necessary. For He knows that "*all have sinned and fall short of the glory of God*" (Romans 3:23). We might break through the fence, or be pushed out of the fold by another, or find ourselves caught between the rocks without the faintest idea of how we got there, but rest assured we will all lose our way at one time or another. And yes, for a time, we may wonder if the shepherd will ever come. We may wait, suffer, and doubt—all the while feeling as though none of it is helping us return to the fold.

But, just maybe, the time between getting lost and rescued is really the most crucial part. While we, unintelligent sheep, are preoccupied with saving ourselves from hardship, the Good Shepherd is most concerned with preparing our hearts to welcome the rescue.

Did the Israelites not wander around the desert for forty years before God brought them into the promised land? Did God not strip away their autonomy that they might learn to trust in Him alone? Were they not hungry and He fed them? Were they not thirsty and He caused water to gush out of a rock? Did He not go before them every single day as a sign that only He knew the way? And did they still doubt? Yes. And, when we go through our own painful desert seasons, we will too. But we have a gift the Israelites did not have access to. We know how the story ends—there is indeed a promised land!

When the Israelites finally reached the land for which they had been waiting, the Lord instructed Joshua to build a monument of stones and declared that these stones would be "*...to the people of Israel a memorial forever*" (Joshua 4:7). The pieces we break always end up being the pieces God uses to remake us into His perfect image. God never wants us to forget His faithfulness in this regard.

Christ's scars are the memorials He uses to remind us of His love—a love always available to us and more than capable of healing our wounded souls. Just as Isaiah foretold, our saviour engraved us on the palms of His hands (Isaiah 46:16) with a visible mark that countless men and women testified to touching and seeing. Christ bore scars because God wanted us to *know* with great assurance what He had done for us. Christ's scars procure hope in uncertain times. Christ's scars affirm His never-failing presence in our lives. Christ's scars secure our future. And like Christ's scars, God wants to use our wounded places to heal us and permanently alter us for His good. Because nothing—no sickness, no death, no injury, no lost relationship—slips through the hands of God. He is in control, working all things together for the good of those who *love* Him (Romans 8:28).

What is good? Running to the open arms of an all-knowing Father is good. Trusting that He is at work in every situation is good. Believing in the hope that all the brokenness will one day be made right, in His timing, is good. And finally, sloughing off our earthly callouses, the part of us that longs to love the world, and allowing God to restore our functionality by first altering our form is good. Each and every time we turn up our palms up to the friend who is doubting herself and God, when we lift our veils and invite her to brush her fingers along our sealed soul skin, we can know that our scars are our own memorials to point others to Christ's love.

Lest we not forget, as we stare down at our altered skin, that our God is a God of abundance. When we open our hands, branded by the mark of His redeeming power to do His good work, He will bless and multiply our usefulness so that many are fed. And we will be left standing in awe at the overflowing baskets where once there was almost nothing.

Chapter Eighteen

built to endure

"Go on," He said.
"How long?" I posed.
"A while," He beckoned,
my will composed.

I strain my eyes
to grasp the view.
"That's mine," He whispered,
"I'm enough for you."

It's 8:00 p.m., that sacred time in our household when my husband and I finally get to sit down together and collapse in a communal exhale. Our kids, who jump and jostle and fight and complain and love and laugh, have finally drifted off into slumberland, and we are afforded the blessed opportunity to look into each others eyes, the windows of one another's souls, and sift through what's lurking there. It's an hour where we sit in the same room and allow the time to unfold, unplanned, unscheduled, with no agenda. Void of effort and intention, this time can easily be swallowed up with our phones or TV shows, but we choose, like the vows wrapped around our fingers and our hearts, to be present, to know one another deeply, and to care.

This night, we sip hot tea and soberly discuss a couple in our small group who are separating. After a break in the conversation, our individual contemplation of the matter causes a battery of questions to linger like smoke in the hushed silence between us.

I notice my husband plucking away at his phone. Before the lull in our conversation, I had asked my husband, the ever-eloquent wordsmith, to craft a message to the small group men to implore them to pray over this heart-breaking situation. Ever the inquirer, I prick the bubble of silence that envelopes us both.

"Are you sending a message now?" I ask.

"Mmmm hmm," he says with his bottom lip half curled, his signature mark of concentration.

As I filter his response, moving it around in my brain to organize and file his expressions, my phone *bings,* and his words surprise me in precisely the same manner as our first kiss. It's quite something to be married to someone for eleven years and still experience moments that catch your breath.

The message that appears in a blue bubble before me is funny and cute, yet dripping with a sincerity for which I should thank God more constantly. You see, my husband calls me ascetic, frugal, or self-sacrificing, depending on the circumstance. Basically, I don't like to spend money on stuff, especially stuff I don't need, which means I am no fashionista and my hair is the same boring shade of brown as your grandfather's loafers, plus or minus a few silver scuff marks.

"I've ordered you the sweater—don't be mad," it reads, because our son is heading off to kindergarten in one short week and our daughter is starting "nastics." There is all sorts of new in our house except for me, who is still at home, still not working, still chained to a broken brain, and still wondering if looking up is considered a step forward in anyone's estimation of life.

I click on the image and a cranberry sweatshirt pops up, the kind you'd slip on after coffee on a wintery Saturday and live quite comfortably in for the rest of the day. The kind of sweater that absorbs hugs and hides stains and doesn't mind being tossed in the dryer along with kids underwear, bath towels, and dozens and dozens of unmatched socks. The words that stretch across the chest cause my lips to slide into a sheepish grin I think I'll fall asleep with—"Built to endure."

I look up past my phone to the one who's seen me bust wide open, broken apart, and crushed. There are no secrets between us, no veils. He has brushed his hands across my scars and felt every puckered ridge, yet every night he says "I do" by the way he prays for my soul while tenderly clasping my hand.

To see all my brokenness and yet name me *built* is to see me through the unveiled eyes of Christ. Because, the truth is, we live in a world that shudders at wounds, that balks at brokenness. We want to live neat, tidy lives on the outside and avoid all casualties. We squint our eyes at the light and keep truth at arm's length because our bend in this mixed up existence will always be to hide our brokenness from each other and God.

I know this tendency all too well; it robbed me of my freedom and shackled me to impossible standards, until I discovered the Jesus of the Bible, whose sole purpose of His earthly life was to break—for me. This mission was so important that He foreshadowed this theme of breaking long before His body broke.

Matthew records one of Christ's most talked about miracles, the feeding of the 5000, in which Jesus is followed by a crowd of people desperate to hear his message and receive his healing, even though He himself is trying to retreat and be alone with God.

Moved with compassion, Jesus responds to the people the only way he knows how, with love, by tending to the sick. After some time, the disciples become concerned because it is getting late and they are in the middle of nowhere and everyone, including the disciples, is hungry. Jesus asks His followers what they have to feed the people, and the disciples respond that only a few fishes and loaves have been accounted for. Once again, humans prove to be insufficient, incapable of solving the problem on their own. And, once again, Jesus takes what little the disciples have, accepts it, and blesses it.

What I often fail to realize in my own life is that Jesus could take a crumb off the ground and make it enough. Jesus always enters into our story where we are, insufficient, and invites us to stand alongside where He has always been, all sufficient, all knowing, all powerful—wholly God.

What follows in the story is often read over quickly as minutiae rather than ruminated on as a profound symbolism for all people. Jesus stands before His disciples with loaves raised and He breaks them (Matthew 14:13–21). Jesus breaks the bread to demonstrate that what happens after the breaking is always miraculous, and it is always much more than we deserve or expect. Chances are, if you've attended Sunday school or picked up a children's Bible or even muddled your way through the book of Matthew on your own, you know how this story ends. Jesus gives the bread back to the disciples, inviting them, inviting us all, to participate in His work. The disciples feed the people until they are satisfied and still there is an excess spilling over. This bread that was broken for them does not just whet their appetite or quell the hungry complainers; it abundantly satisfies them.

In 2013, shortly after our son was born, I experienced a holy moment while privately worshipping God. I was on my knees in the shower, unclothed physically and spiritual before God, lifting my hands in surrender as an act of granting Him unimpaired access to my soul. At the time, I did not fully comprehend the significance of this surrender or what it would mean in the following years. I did not know that, after this declaration of great joy and trust in Him, I would experience significant sorrow and doubt. With the naivety of an immature disciple, I thought I could confidently straddle surrender and the desire for earthly blessing. This is still widely preached and yet Jesus' own life renders it grossly untrue. Genuine surrender almost always involves a great earthly crushing.

The grapes must be stomped upon, the olives pressed down, and the disciples broken to appreciate and receive her anointing. Knowing this, we needn't ever fear the desert, or the storm, or whatever terrifying act brings about our earthly crushing. Christ demonstrates that we were created to faithfully endure the breaking, that we may gratefully receive His anointing. We may feel pressed down on every side, perplexed, and abandoned, yet it is precisely in these excruciating moments when He is doing his best work of extraction in us. When the crushing is complete, when our own will has been broken against the absolute sovereignty of His, an abundance of pure faith will surely pour out.

The way in which God does the crushing is as unique as the disciple it is meant to transform. In my circumstance, God used my physical body to reveal the dysfunctional state of my soul and disillusioned view of Him. For some time, I did not know what was causing my physical pain. I couldn't see into my body and locate the brokenness. It took the examination of a specialist, of an outsider looking in, to diagnose the problem. And once He did—it changed my life. I began to understand that my functionality was completely dependent on acknowledging my brokenness. This was true of my physical body and oh how truer still it has been with my soul.

I have just returned from my three months check-in with the neurologist. Thanks be to God for His intercessional power—things are considerably better than before. I have less anxiety, tension, and pain than I once did, and I feel hope for my body's future even though the wiring in my brain remains broken, along with other earthly dreams. Yet, I can say with absolute confidence that the price I have paid in physical suffering pales in comparison to the miraculous healing work God has done to transform my soul.

Many of you reading this story have experienced the crack of hard pavement and subsequent pain much more excruciating than mine. You know all too well the seriousness of the collision between souls created for wholeness and a world marred by sin. If this is where you find yourself today, please do not believe the lie that you have been abandoned. The pain you are experiencing in the secret places behind your veils is never hidden from God. His veil has already been torn. Jesus' death on the cross not only removed the barrier of separation between us and Him, it granted us direct access to the healing balm needed to bind and close the deepest wounds of our souls—God's love.

My story is but one account of many, recorded across time and nations, that bears witness to the miracle of an unveiled soul encountering His everlasting love and subsequent healing that leaves one forever marked with a holy scar. These scars, like Christ's, serve as a permanent branding to remind us that "...We are more sinful and flawed in ourselves than we ever dared believe, yet at the very same time we are more loved and accepted in Jesus Christ than we ever dared hope."[39]

Paul, who suffered more wounds, physically and spiritually, than the sum of five of our own life times, was a man who was beaten, mocked, stoned, jailed, and eventually killed for his faith. This man, who's soul was splintered by his own denial, his own blindness of who Christ really was, poses the question meant to forever rouse us from our deepest fear—that we have been abandoned in our current condition. He says, "*Who shall separate us from the love of Christ? Shall tribulation, or distress, or persecution, or famine, or nakedness, or danger, or sword?*" (Romans 8:35).

And based on his own soul's collision with Christ, his own personal unravelling and unveiling, he confidently replies, "*No, in all these things we are more than conquerors through him who loved us*" (Romans 8:37).

We are more than conquerors. We are built to endure. The pain of shattered earthly dreams, unmet expectations, and the waiting, the painful, prolonged waiting, is only temporary. In light of this truth, we are invited to live in a broken world, healed and fully surrendered to Christ. Because, one day, our enduring souls will rise and every one of our fault lines, lovingly filled in by grace, will glisten in the light of God's glory. On that blissful day, when Jesus runs His hands along the puckered ridges of our scars, we will realize that these holy marks, this evidence of our collision with Christ on our short journey home, have only made our arrival all the more sweet. And we will praise the God of Abraham, Isaac, and Jacob for wrestling with us—and winning.

endnotes

1 "Scar," *Wikipedia, accessed March 26, 2019, https://en.wikipedia.org/wiki/Scar.*

2 "The Hip is the Largest, Strongest Joint in the Human Body," *Functional Spine and Sport, accessed March 26, 2019, https://functionalspineandsport.com/patient-education/2018/7/9/the-hip-is-the-largest-strongest-joint-in-the-human-body.*

3 Anahad O'Connor, "The Claim: After Being Broken, Bones Can Become Even Stronger," *The New York Times, accessed March 26, 2019, https://www.nytimes.com/2010/10/19/health/19really.html.*

4 Dinah Maria Mulock Craik, *A Life for a Life (New York, N.Y.: Harper and Brothers, 1877), 169*, quoted in Timothy Keller, *The Meaning of Marriage: Facing the Complexities of Commitment with the Wisdom of God* (New York, N.Y.: Riverhead Books, 2011), 122.

5 "Capacity of Bridges," *Government of Canada, accessed March 26, 2019, https://www.tc.gc.ca/eng/railsafety/guideline-731.htm.*

6 John Piper, *A Peculiar Glory* (Wheaton, Ill.: Crossway. 2016), 16.

7 "Eating Disorders," *National Institute of Mental Health*, March 25, 2019, https://www.nimh.nih.gov/health/topics/eating-disorders/index.shtml

8 C. S. Lewis, *The Complete C. S. Lewis Signature Classics: Mere Christianity; The Screwtape Letters; The Abolition of Man; The Great Divorce; The Problem of Pain; Miracles; A Grief Observed* (New York, N.Y.: HarperOne, 2002), 506.

9 Katherine Wolf & Jay Wolf, *Hope Heals: A True Story of Overwhelming Loss and an Overcoming Love* (Grand Rapids: Zondervan, 2016), 191.

10 Alan Fogel, "Emotional and Physical Pain Activate Similar Brain Regions," *Psychology Today, accessed March 26, 2019, https://www.*

psychologytoday.com/ca/blog/body-sense/201204/emotional-and-physical-pain-activate-similar-brain-regions.

11 "Augustine (354–430 C.E.)," *Internet Encyclopedia of Philosophy, accessed December 14, 2019, https://www.iep.utm.edu/augustin/.*

12 Augustine, *Confessions: A New Translation by Sarah Ruden, (*New York, N.Y.: Penguin, 2017), 43.

13 "Foothold," *Merriam-Webster, accessed March 26, 2019, https://www.merriam-webster.com/dictionary/foothold.*

14 Augustine, *Confessions: A New Translation by Sarah Ruden*, 35.

15 *"Let," Lexico, accessed March 26, 2019, https://www.lexico.com/definition/let.*

16 *Kristen Domonell,* "Why endorphins (and exercise) make you happy," *CNN, accessed March 26, 2019, https://www.cnn.com/2016/01/13/health/endorphins-exercise-cause-happiness/index.html.*

17 "Dr. Paul Brand CBE," *The Leprosy Mission, accessed March 26, 2019, https://www.leprosymission.org.uk/about-us-and-leprosy/our-history/paul-brand.aspx.*

18 Jean-Marie Cavanihac, "Fishes and Scales," *Microscopy–UK*, accessed March 26, 2019, *http://www.microscopy-uk.org.uk/mag/indexmag.html?http://www.microscopy-uk.org.uk/mag/artjan02/fishes.html.*

19 American Chemical Society, "Solving The Mystery Of The Metallic Sheen Of Fish," *Science Daily*, accessed March 26, 2019, *https://www.sciencedaily.com/releases/2008/01/080114100008.htm.*

20 "Brother Lawrence: Practitioner of God's Presence," *Christianity Today, accessed December 14, 2019,* https://www.christianitytoday.com/history/people/innertravelers/brother-lawrence.html.

21 Ibid.

22 Brother Lawrence, *The Practice of the Presence of God*, (Boston, MA.: New Seeds, 2005), 5.

23 Ibid., 46.

24 Hobart M. King, "Basalt: What is Basalt, How does it Form, and How is it Used?," *Geology.com, accessed March 26, 2019, https://geology.com/rocks/basalt.shtml.*

25 A. W. Tozer, *The Essential Tozer Collection: The Pursuit of God; The Purpose of Man; The Crucified Life*, ed. James L. Snyder (Bloomington, MN: Bethany House Publishers, 2013), 48.

26 Ibid., 49.

27 Augustine, *Confessions: A New Translation by Sarah Ruden,* 184.

28 Ibid., 37

29 Louis Bouyer, *A History of Christian Spirituality* (New York, N.Y.: Seabury, 1982), 313, quoted in Dallas Willard, *The Spirit of the Disciplines: Understanding How God Changes Lives* (New York, N.Y.: Harper Collins, 1988), 161.

30 Richard Foster, *Celebrations of Discipline* (New York, N.Y.: HarperOne, 1998), 101.

31 "Guide to the Attributes of God," *Zondervan Academic, accessed March 26, 2019, https://zondervanacademic.com/blog/attributes-of-god/.*

32 Augustine, *Confessions: A New Translation by Sarah Ruden,* 173.

33 Willard, *The Spirit of the Disciplines: Understanding How God Changes Lives*, 185.

34 Lee Strobel, *The Case for Christ* (Grand Rapids, M.I.: Zondervan, 2016), 291.

35 Barbara Brown Taylor, *Learning to Walk in the Dark* (New York, N.Y.: Harper Collins, 2014), 162.

36 Annie J. Flint, "He Giveth More Grace," *Timeless Truths Free Online Library, accessed March 26, 2019, https://library.timelesstruths.org/music/He_Giveth_More_Grace/.*

37 Stefano Carnazzi, "Kintsugi: the art of precious," *Lifegate*, accessed December 14, 2019, https://www.lifegate.com/people/lifestyle/kintsugi.

38 Paul E. Miller, *A Praying Life: Connecting with God in a Distracting World (Colorado Springs, C.O.: NavPress, 2009), 12.*

39 Keller, *The Meaning of Marriage*, 44.